"In this exceptional book, Ondrea uses the depth of her mind and heart to heal her body and finds, in her suffering, compassion."
—Ram Dass, author of *Be Here Now* and *Still Here*

"Ondrea Levine's book reveals her courageous willingness to face the inner linings of her heart and the fearful caverns of her ego-mind. The honesty and transparency of her self-exploration is filled with a sensitivity, grace, gentleness, and wisdom that represents the One. Ondrea paves the way for the reader to follow her in an amazing commitment to a uniquely beautiful journey of the heart. This book is truly a love story of how two extraordinary people become one heart as they face the challenges of illness, pain, and death—not seeing them as enemies, but as an exploration of their way to freedom."
—Gerald. G. Jampolsky, M.D., founder of Attitudinal Healing; Diane V. Cirincione, Ph.D., CEO of Attitudinal Healing International

"A beautiful story told in Ondrea's unmistakable voice. This is a deeply personal memoir, but it is also much more than that—it is enlightening and heart opening. Stephen and Ondrea are wonderful teachers with unusual insights and great gifts to bestow upon us."
—Sharon Salzberg, author of *Lovingkindness* and *Real Happiness*

"I read this wise and loving journal avidly, with deep gratitude and delight. These intimate old Dharma friends share how broken hearts, nakedly encountering death and mortality, can catalyze open hearts and selfless service. Their grace-full co-meditations and very special brand of partner spirituality will edify and enrich us all."
—Lama Surya Das, author of *Awakening the Buddha Within* and *Buddha Standard Time*

"Like any skilled translator of the timeless mystics, Stephen Levine captures the essence of his beloved's wild mind and luminous heart. Interweaving her own story with perennial teachings on mindfulness practice and devotional yogas, Ondrea Levine offers us passages of breathtaking beauty and uncompromising truth-telling, transcending convention and delivering a potent dose of dharma directly to the spiritual bloodstream. This book is an inoculation, a profound healing."

—Mirabai Starr, author of *God of Love*

"I have been a huge fan of Stephen and Ondrea Levine's work for many years. Their deep, healing and transformative teachings have had a profound impact on my life. They are authentic teachers of great wisdom and heart."

—Marci Shimoff, *New York Times* best-selling author of *Happy for No Reason*

"What a story! And how amazing it seemed as I followed the growth or maturation or . . . expansion of mind and spirit of someone already so obviously ready, 33 years ago, to hop aboard the same spiritual train where you were punching tickets."

—Lee Quarnstrom, writer-practitioner-prankster

"Rarely are we offered the privilege of sharing in the rigorously honest, humbly genuine, and deeply authentic inner pilgrimage of another human being. This is the story of how Ondrea was shaped by a symphony of forces—broken open by people, events and winds that blew both harsh and gentle; punishing and uplifting; through darkness and light. Ondrea is a gift to us all. She shares remarkable clarity, insight and counsel for us to hold dear, to cherish, and to pass on to those souls brave enough to follow Love wherever it may take."

—Wayne Muller, best-selling author of *Sabbath* and
A Life of Being, Having, and Doing Enough

"This book is an enheartening masterpiece. I have never felt my heart so close to the surface when reading a book. Ondrea Levine is living proof that grace is not something that pours down from the heavens; it is something that rises up from within us. Reading her story is a blessing not in disguise. This book is the perfect preparation for an enheartened life."

—Jeff Brown, author of *Soulshaping: A Journey of Self-Creation*

The steadfast union of Ondrea and Stephen that forged a path of healing for so many over the past decades now takes us on an unparalleled inner journey. Her story offers guidance for all those who have been wounded in life, and all those who strive to keep their hearts open. Life events alternating with poetic teachings catalyze both the mind and spirit. Wise, touching, tender and pure, her generosity and honesty will be a source of inspiration for all.

—Francine Shapiro, Ph.D., originator of EMDR therapy,
author of *Getting Past Your Past*

"We have been patiently waiting for *The Healing I Took Birth For*. It is a deeply inspiring account of a life devoted to healing and compassionate service. This beautiful book is filled with grace, love, and humanity. Like a pearl diver, Ondrea dives deep in her own wounds to find the gift that can serve others."

—Frank Ostaseski, founder of the Metta Institute

"For decades, Ondrea and Stephen have offered themselves in selfless service to all beings who seek a way home within. Once again, they freely share the intimacies of their lives as *dharmic* teaching for us all. In telling her story, Ondrea validates and elucidates the path of transforming pain into peace. Ondrea's story is one of her awakening to the beauty of her True Nature. It is also a love story of how the two hearts of Ondrea and Stephen beat as One Heart."

—Paula Whang-Ramos, M.Div., Ph.D., psychologist, minister at Center for Spiritual Enlightenment; Rich Ramos, R.N., M.S., Pediatric Oncology Nurse at Lucile Packard Children's Hospital

"Absorbing these vital heart waves of one life. Congratulations on rotating the axis of the universe. Still quivering."

—Gary Gach, Buddhist teacher, author, and translator

"As a hospice physician who deals with illness and impending death, I have learned, from Ondrea, the difference between curing the body and healing the shared heart. Ondrea has touched the lives of so many people, and this book will extend her healing work from those who have experienced her compassionate presence to those who will get to know her through her open-hearted words. She is an inspiration to me and to countless others who have been graced by her teachings."

—Fred Schwartz, M.D.

"In *The Healing I Took Birth For,* Stephen not only autobiographically accounts Ondrea's life, her selfless service, bouts with illnesses, writings, workshops and more, but takes their teachings to a more intimate place than ever before. Through implementing the insights, wisdom, and knowledge shared in *The Healing I Took Birth For,* I can unequivocally say that I am a better human being because of it."

—Chris Grosso, *www.TheIndieSpiritualist.com*

The Healing
I Took Birth For

Practicing the Art of Compassion

Ondrea Levine

as told to Stephen Levine

WEISERBOOKS
San Francisco, CA / Newburyport, MA

This revised edition first published in 2015 by Weiser Books, an imprint of
Red Wheel/Weiser, LLC
With offices at:
665 Third Street, Suite 400
San Francisco, CA 94107
www.redwheelweiser.com

ISBN: 978-1-57863-563-4

Library of Congress Cataloging-in-Publication Data available upon request.

Cover design by Jim Warner
Cover photograph © Granadilla, watercolor on paper. Ehret, Georg Dionysius
(1710-70) © The Right Hon. Earl of Derby / Bridgeman Images
Interior by Frame25 Productions
Typeset in Garamond Premier Pro

PRINTED IN CANADA
MP
10 9 8 7 6 5 4 3 2 1

*Many of the poems by Stephen embedded in Ondrea's story, in an attempt to per-
sonify her initiations and insights in the course of her process, previously appeared
in a few earlier books and periodicals.*

Dedication

To my beloved Stephen's heart, the kindest I have ever known.

Thank you to Tara for her acceptance, vivaciousness, charm, and love. Thank you to Noah for his playful nature, contagious laugh, openness and love. And to his wife, kind Amy, who brought bright-eyed baby Hazel and Stevie Ray into the midst.

Thank you to James for his quick wit, forgiveness, and love. And infinite blessings to Danielle, Gilbert, Mariah, and Peyton, our grandchildren, for bringing more play, laughter, and love into our lives.

"Fortunate" does not come close to expressing my gratitude for having met Stephen and being inside each other's process for more than thirty-seven years. I know this is equally true for him, because I just asked him to write this down.

Because of Stephen's love for me, this book makes me seem a bit more wholehearted than I may be. I am honored, though a little taken aback, by his vision of me. What is closest to the truth is that I have learned to love and am unendingly grateful to his gift for writing about our shared process of learning and the healing that goes beyond the body.

In the Ramayana, Laxshman sat by the River Jumna and reflected on his life, saying, "It was like something I dreamed once; long ago and far away."

Contents

"Embracing" • Photo by C. Gallo

Acknowledgments

Thanks to encouraging friends, I hold close to my heart:

Susan Barber
Linda Barrett
Dale Borglum
Roy Brown
Gregg Cassin
Ram Dass
Sita de Leeuw
Flyingfish
Chris George
Garry George
Wavy Gravy
Tara Goleman & Daniel Goleman
Soren Gordhamer
Jeff "R.P." Harbour
Charles Horowitz
Barbara Iannoli
Gerald Jampolsky & Diane Cirincione
Richard Johnson
Allen Klein
Jack Kornfield
Jai Lakshman

Leandro Lopez & Nancy Lopez

Arthur Martin

Fred Schwartz & Lewis Miller

Wayne Muller

Belleruth Naparstek

Ron Polte & Sally Polte

Paula Wang Ramos & Rich Ramos

Sharon Salzberg

Francine Shapiro

Mirabai Starr

Christine Tiernan

Nanette Tafoya

Jai Uttal

John Welshon

Dawn Yun

Claudia Yunker & Richard "Preacher" Yunker

Noami Atencio (our divine Postmaster)

And a deep bow to publisher and visionary Jan Johnson and editor Gary Leon Hill, and the fine eye of Michael Alexander, who brought the work to fruition.

And much thanks to Gizmo productions, Kevyn Gilbert, Max Moulton, and Destin Moulton, professional website developers (*www.gizmoproductions.com*), producers of the ongoing healing and meditation website, *www.LevineTalks.com,* which includes The Apology Page, an experiment in compassion and forgiveness for all who wish to participate. It was created and is maintained with considerable grace by Ondrea.

Great thanks to Chris Gallo for phenomenal photography.

Healing Team

Maria Saranteas, O.D., whose extraordinary healing energy is a regular blessing

Fred Schwartz, M.D., who has been our loving, trusted friend for many years

Dr. Karen LoRusso, a kind, local oncologist

Dr. Timothy Call, a kind Mayo CLL specialist

The most informative leukemia Internet sites:

www.cllcanada.ca (Christopher Dwyer)

www.facebook.com/groups/CLLSupport (on Facebook, bad to the bone)

www.clltopics.org (Chaya Venkat)

www.acor.org

www.ralphmossblog.com/p/moss-reports.html (Ralph Moss, M.D.; excellent information on cancers)

For video and audio tapes of Ondrea and Stephen's talks and meditations, contact: *www.WarmRockTapes.com*

Introduction by Stephen Levine

Ondrea and I have collaborated on the heart-breaking/heart-healing task of putting a life of suffering and grace into the conceits and corruptions of language. Exploring her inner experiences and the events that marked her unfolding, we attempted to speak from our shared perception of the process of her healing. Not just the curing of the body, but the healing of the heart, the finishing of unfinished business.

This is the most intimate collaboration of any we have worked on. It afforded an opportunity to be within each other's experience in a most remarkable way. Nothing short of grace allowed me to be able to write her story in her first person singular.

I may have been something of a teacher to Ondrea for our first few years together. But having traversed the narrow corridors and open spaces through which she passed, she had already come to the surface, demonstrating a deeply compassionate knowing of what people want and need—a healer's knowing. She came with knowledge of how to use what remains hidden as a means of calling forth who we really are.

Coming into her own, she prevailed against fear and forgetfulness, which limits our growth and healing. Learning out loud, she transmitted what the sad old Russian poet said, "That which is unloved, decomposes quickly." And she became my teacher for the dozens of years to follow.

This book is the result of her explorations along the pathways to her true and original nature. It's an experiment in consciousness to find in "the numbness" of the past, a clarity she never imagined possible.

She calls these autobiographical glimpses, these milestones on the path of her evolution, a love story. Her method was to draw the illusive past up from the stream of consciousness as best she could, mindful that emotion can sometimes attenuate time, leaving the past a little vague, and that memory can be more like a painting than a photograph, able to distort the moments she was attempting to portray.

She first compiled a life list and then began to flesh out some of her experiences. Having had difficulty throughout her life with a repeatedly interruptive kind of slurred thought, she asked me to find the words that told our story.

Because I have been happily present for the second half of her life, I was able to include stories she had forgotten. For us, it was a "mystical union." The synapse between hearts breeched in such an extraordinary manner that it allowed her feelings, notations, and insights to find their way into these words, to speak through me for the healing of something in us all.

It was uncanny how at times it seemed as though I knew her as well as myself and could approximate her inner experience—the shared heart able to give expression to some of her deepest feelings as she had, through the years, been able to give voice to mine.

Though many of our "unusual" experiences were similar—in fact in some cases exactly the same—I was honored to tell the story of the precarious life which she saved like a stranger from drowning.

As she said, rereading this manuscript, "I know this is all true, but as I read this it all seems like fiction to me."

Fever Dream

I walked through half my life
as if it were a fever dream

barely touching the ground

my eyes half open, my heart half closed.

Not half knowing who I was
I watched the ghost of me
drift from room to room
through friends and lovers
never quite as real as advertised.

Not saying half I meant or meaning half I said
I dreamed myself from birth to birth
seeing some true self.

Until the fever broke
and my heart could not abide
a moment longer,
as the rest of me awoke,
summoned from the dream,
not half caring for anything but love.

ONE

What's Happening?

I WAS A CHILD OF WARFARE.

My father married my mother, his high school sweetheart, after he graduated from college, just before he was drafted. She wanted to get pregnant before they shipped him off, but he was quite practical about the unknown and promised if he survived that would be "the first thing" they would do when he got home.

My father, an unworldly orthodox Jew from the Bronx, landed with an army of reinforcements on the shores of Normandy six weeks after the D-Day massacre. "It was like death's junkyard," he said. The grotesque wreckage of men's courage and death-dealing machinery was plowed aside so the trucks could get "the new meat" up to the front.

Pushing against the Nazis, who killed Jewish boys when they were captured, and even called "Jew boy" by one of his own, my father fought his way across Europe without a chance to wash or change clothes for months. Like the rest of the division, his rifle never leaving his hands, he fired toward those who fired at him, turning his German counterparts—college boys like him—into letters to be delivered on their mothers' *strasse* (street).

They fought their way toward the Rhine until they hit the Herzberg Woods, advancing from tree to tree for months, through thick winter fog. Muzzle blasts showed the target, and to fire back was to become the next target. It was death fighting death in the damp stink of blood and earth. No place for a nice Jewish boy.

And when they broke through, my father recalled, "the general himself pinned medals on us all and said we deserved a break. Sent up north to a quiet area near the Ardennes Forest for a bit of R&R," he and his best friend, a Hispanic fellow also from the Bronx, washed, changed clothes, and breathed their first natural breaths in months.

Just before sunrise on an overcast, wintry day, an artillery burst from the "defeated East" and the snort and rattle of the panzers came crashing through the woods. Hitler's last *putsch*, "the Battle of the Bulge," killed most of my father's company immediately and many of the rest over the next three days. His whole regiment was without winter gear and barely equipped for battle, rifles against tanks, ammunition quickly running low. The northern European winter froze them in their foxholes. He always spoke of the cold. He was cold until he died.

The old Belgian village they had hoped to fall back to in order to regroup got caught from behind in a pincer-type military movement. His lines collapsed as they pulled back. Crossing a stone bridge with a few of his comrades, the Nazi soldiers close behind, he knelt and kept firing until his clips were exhausted.

When he found out later that besides the combat rifleman's medal, he had also been awarded two bronze stars, he wondered who had put him up for the awards. "I didn't think that sergeant even knew I stayed behind to cover their retreat."

Hours later, they reached the Mobile Army Medical Hospital behind the lines and sat dazed in the surreal stillness with the angry overture of cannon fire in the distance. They had to check themselves to see if they were really alive. It is said that many, even all these years later, are still not sure.

At the end of the war, General Eisenhower said something to the effect that one of the greatest tragedies of war is the silence that follows, the inability to express the horrors they had experienced or the part of themselves they had left on the battle field. For the rest of his life, my father did not like any loud noise or show of emotion, not even talking. He became the silence General Eisenhower predicted would be the cruel legacy of such a horrific hardship.

Displaying a tension just beneath the surface, he was mostly mute. He never had a normal conversation with anyone but his wife or a complete stranger. Normally, he simply turned and walked away.

> *A turmoil of wars—men spread over the middle kingdom*
> *Three hundred and sixty thousand.*
> *And sorrow, sorrow like rain.*
> *Sorrow to go, and sorrow, sorrow returning.*
> *Desolate, desolate fields*
> *And no children of war upon them.*
> —Li Po (translated by Ezra Pound)

Three years after he left, my father came home, and I was the fulfillment of his promise to my mother. He had barely survived the Battle of the Bulge, and it seems that he passed that hyper-vigilant, survival consciousness on to me.

I was born in December under a distant star. No welcome mat. Even the Magi were afraid to enter. They just dropped their fear and confusion on the doorstep and made a quick getaway. I thought I was left at the wrong address.

Isolation

I think my parents really wanted a child, but that was as far as it went. They must have ordered a different model; they never seemed satisfied with the one they got.

There seemed to be something missing. I was never sure I was welcome. Looking out between the bars in my playpen, seldom being picked up or touched, I watched my mother nap away the day. I look back at this time and wonder if I am somewhat like that monkey in the lab, about which so much is written in scientific journals. Was I being tested to see how well I could do without affection? I started to contract my mother's depression.

What could I have done in some previous existence? Perhaps I was being punished for taking birth, with another forty lashes for not being a boy. My parents didn't seem to act the same way with my two younger brothers. I lived at the edges of a family, in a middle class neighborhood, on a rural country road, on the face of an uncertain world. I was alone at the edge of a silent, unemotional world in which touching, speaking, and laughing were prohibited. Everyone had their own room; we were compartmentalized in so many ways.

It was reading, the contact with great minds, that offered me a lifeline when confusion was at its greatest. Though it was quite difficult to read sometimes, due to a condition yet to be diagnosed—the lines floated on the page, words shifted and moved. For years I rode my bike and read alone all day. Books were my life, my best friends, and my teachers. I found them much easier to relate to than people. I had little of what I'd call a social life.

I danced with myself, in the space between breaths. I lay on my back and watched the night sky revolving around me. I was the still center of the universe around which all motion turned. I watched the stars constellate into figments of my imagination. It was obvious that the mind had a mind of its own.

Although I was practicing the art of being alone, I did not realize at the time that I was also preparing the foundation of the meditation practice I would learn decades later.

When I spoke to my mother, it was often met with tension. I think my scrambled mind drove her crazy. I have come to understand how this might drive any parent to distraction. It was quite clear that I was in the way and she resented it. If I did anything with a dyslexic tinge, from counting change to confusing directions or trying to explain something about myself, she would grimace and say, "I could just kill you." I was always hyper-alert when she was around. I never knew what she might do next.

Once I was grabbed by some neighborhood boys and hung like a piñata by my ankles in my garage as an object of ridicule. When my mother came out and saw what was happening, she just laughed and went back into the house. The boys let me down, but some part of me was left hanging there.

I felt so isolated within the family that it seemed like a good idea to take my pulse every once in a while just to make sure I was still alive. At times I was overwhelmed by a free-floating sadness, a grief for which I could find no reason. I felt as though someone had died. But where was the corpse?

When I was ten, I was dropped off at the doctor's office for an infected splinter in my thumb. Alone in that strange, peculiar-smelling, wood-paneled office, I was told to take off all my clothes and lie naked on the long white table. I can still feel the doctor's cold hands and very strange eyes on my body. I walked home swearing I would never go to a doctor again!

When puberty arrived, it just added to my confusion. I got my period in social studies class in the eighth grade. I went to the school nurse, and she called my mother to pick me up. Not a word was said, but the next day there was a giant box of Kotex on the first stair to my room and a bra a few steps further up. If anyone ever needed some kind of "adolescent body class," it was me. I wished I was invisible.

In my dreams, my long undiagnosed dyslexia left me disoriented and frightened. I felt like I would never find my way home. Sometimes I feared I might get lost in school because I couldn't remember how to get to class. I was no less lost in my waking world.

When one is raised in a home that lacks loving touch or playful interactions, it may leave a sense of something missing. As a child grows, there may develop a faceless confusion, unfulfilled longing, a far-reaching grief that may leave hollow places, and feelings of something being absent. As an adult, that child may feel a fear of parenting or a trepidation of opening to their "inner child" that can't be explained. It's a breaking of their inner compass that leaves them with a disrupted sense of direction, producing a feeling of being lost in the world.

Since my parents spoke very little, to try to get some connection, some understanding, I watched my parents' body language very closely, noting their most minute mannerisms. I think this vocabulary of twitches, blinking, tensions around the jaw and mouth, movements of the shoulders, etc., said more to me than the vocabulary available to me at that age. There was more communicated in the angle of a head than there was in words. I learned the language of emotional expression very quickly. What I deciphered mostly was their pain.

I felt if no one could see me, no one would judge me. Acting invisible became a necessary talent. I should have been a magician's assistant, put in a box, who was then nowhere to be found. But who was the magician? Who could tell me who I was or where I was going? That was when I turned to God. Perhaps, He might have some answers!

I learned much later that others with similar perceptual quirks learned how to communicate from their own families, but because there was so little speaking in my home, I eventually entered the outside world with almost no friends. It is from this dysfunction that I have come to believe many have to leave home to find their real family.

Lost and Found

I used to think I lived among the dead. Self-pity. I used to say I was born in a morgue. Then I stopped saying that because I didn't want to give morgues a bad name. That was before I discovered my parents' history. Which of course I never knew because talking about oneself in our house was prohibited.

A heart-opening instance of interruptive *karma*, when one force interrupts the course of a previous force, occurred when I was eleven and had to go stay at my mother's sister's home while my parents went on vacation. It was an intercessory change.

Aunt Bernice

I had never met Aunt Bernice before. She lived deep in the sprawling city of Brooklyn. I only stayed with her for two weeks, but it made a life-long impression on my heart.

I was excited, and a bit fearful. She was a very kind and loving woman. Her sweetness took me aback for a few moments, but when she wrapped her loving arms around me, she took me into another world. We sat together on the old, overstuffed couch and talked and drank cocoa until it was time for bed.

She was open and sharing. She began to fill me in on the traumatic influences my parents had endured which she felt might ease my pain and help me not take some of their actions so personally. She was surprised that I did not know their wounds. She told me how my mother had refused to see her estranged mother when she was dying, how it seemed she never forgave anyone in her life.

My mother had been an intelligent little girl, bubbling away as many two-year-olds do, and then her mother ran off with another man. Her loving father, a wealthy businessman, took care of her and her sister until he died when she was eleven. Aunt Bernice told me my mother was then given to her father's sister and her husband, who had four children, and were given her father's business, which they soon lost because of their lack of business acumen. My mother resented them for losing her "wealth."

My mother met my father in high school and married him right after she graduated. That same year he finished college. Both were staunch liberals. She was eighteen, he was twenty-two.

As I now have learned their story, he went to war, and after he returned, I came along. I think having a child was more than she bargained for. She began to withdraw, disappearing into her "who-done-its," and dozing most of the day until my father came home from work.

My parents were perfect for each other; cocooned against interruption. I thought of them as Cinderella and Prince Charming in a storybook I had to read alone in my room. They liked the idea of children more than having children. And it seemed that a girl child really broke my mother's "glass slipper." It occurred to me sometime later that perhaps her aversion to a female child may have had something to do with the female person who betrayed her so early on.

Considering their wounds, my parents did the best they could. Given what providence had bestowed on them, through no fault of their own, I think if they created "bad" karma by not wanting to touch or feel another person, they did it because they saw no alternative. It was just the closest they could get without mirroring their own pain.

Aunt Bernice told me how my father loved jazz. He was exceptionally liberal and generous and went to the Apollo Theater in Harlem before he was sent off to war. She showed me photos of him smiling, back in those days before the tragedy of war. After he returned, she said, "only a still-life remained."

Aunt Bernice spoke of her own wounds as well. She told me that she had been a kindergarten teacher but had to give up "her children" because lupus disease had forced her to retire. She said she could never have children of her own because, as a young woman, when she was nine months' pregnant, she was in an automobile accident that killed her unborn baby and left her unable to reproduce. She said that after this traumatic event most of her life was centered on service. I asked her what "service" meant, and she said it was "helping others" and that it made her feel really good, a worthwhile person. Her neighbor's children called her Aunt Bunny.

She reminded me of a quote from Helen Keller: "The most beautiful things in the world cannot be seen or even touched, they must be felt with the heart."

I gave this a lot of thought. Service felt like such a natural way to live. She had put my little locomotive on the right track. I loved the weeks with her and their beneficial influence on my life. It was my first little teaching in *karma*, the law of momentum that pushes our life along, displaying to us that whatever comes our way, good or bad, pleasant or unpleasant, if we are not mindful, we tend to pass it on. I wanted to pass goodness along. She was the seed and the motivation for this, and I often send blessings out to her.

Besides telling me of Helen Keller, Aunt Bernice also gave me the book Anne Frank's *The Diary of a Young Girl,* which introduced me to a courageous, loving Judaism I never knew existed. And she read to me from Martin Buber's *Tales of the Hasidism,* which contains a deep love and wisdom, a humor and compassion I didn't know was part of my legacy. We spoke of how many were confused, even Jews themselves, about what was meant when it is said, to the consternation and animosity of many people, that Jews were the "Chosen People." It seemed the misunderstanding of that had brought great suffering down on their heads from people who thought the Jews were saying they were better than everyone else, who thought perhaps we even had it easier than all others. But that could not be further from the truth. It actually means we may have it harder because we were chosen in the Testament to be true to the Law no matter how painful or difficult, to be righteous even when an easier alternative might be available. We may not be the most glorious, but sometimes the most wretched, struggling to keep love in a heart that might otherwise be tempted by anger and hate. There may even be the tendency toward revenge, which can so easily distract us from what the Buddha called, and every spiritual hero echoes, "the work to be done."

I found it hard to believe that Bernice and my mother were related. After their mother died, my mother felt her wounds, and Bernice, because of the kindness of the family who took her in, took a different path.

Bernice became my role model for kindness.

Dance and the Approach to God

By the time I was fifteen, dance was a major part of my life. Music filled me. My bedroom was the ballroom. Naturally the blues suited me all too well. It was the first time I could bring the pain to the surface and dance with it. Some thought I was shy; others thought just the opposite, that I was a "show off" because I loved to dance. At school dances everyone watched me act out my feelings of invisibility.

I went to many dances by myself. I was asked to dance but never made friends and always ended up going home alone. I was chosen as the best dancer in my high school. I really enjoyed dancing most when Tina Turner sang her heart out into mine; she said it all for me!

Tina eventually broke loose from her abuser much as I broke loose from mine; hers was a violent husband, mine was the hapless mind itself. Looking like she could knock out Lucifer himself, Tina shattered limitation after limitation. Coming out the other end she sang her ass off. Sometimes I thought perhaps I could hear *the* song in *her* song.

Here, too, in measuring early blessings of power and frenzied grace, I must bow to Janice Joplin who acted as my therapist and much later supported my exploration of Primal Scream.

One day, my dad walked by the living room where I was dancing alone to the Beatles and Trini Lopez. He slipped right up and under my arched arms and began to dance with me. I was quite surprised and delighted. He had seen me dancing by myself and just opened his arms to show me how couples dance. He told me to step up onto his shoes. We danced for a few minutes and then stopped abruptly as if he awoke from a dream. He stepped away, as usual, without a word and went upstairs.

Difficult as it was, the sharp twists and dead spots that the family dynamic presented had their advantages. Since they didn't want me around much when I was a teenager, I had access to their car most of the time. Because interaction was not encouraged in the house—no touching, no laughing, no loud sounds—it was an uncomfortably toxic environment. My father was a buyer of women's coats for a major department store. Rather than speak to me, he brought me gifts: very costly winter coats, a new dress for every dance, and the newest design summer dresses. He so wanted to be alive again, but the war had done him in.

I grew up a chameleon, taking on protective coloring, merging with my environment so as not to become prey. Not just prey to the confusing elements in my world, but most certainly prey to my self-rejection, my hatred of me, "the thinker." If I could have silenced my mind, I would have disappeared into the wallpaper!

Later, when I first read about self-awareness, it gave me a chill. And I wondered if I was going to get lost in my same old self-denial, my hatred of who I was and seemed unable to be otherwise. Prayer helped me be more comfortable in my skin, but clearly it was love that needed to do the job.

Self-hatred is a catalyst for pain, turning it to suffering. Sending hatred rather than mercy into our body, imbalance tips us over, and like a turtle on its back, we paddle the air looking for some way to regain our ground. We bargain with our shame. I could not display my pain to my family because I feared what would be returned would be a wintry blast, backs turned, a dead silence. The only one I could trust was Jesus.

I begged God to make me normal, to understand, to feel my pain so I might feel his compassion. Gradually my self-awareness grew into a slow self-acceptance of even those places of non-acceptance.

How do I accept the unacceptable in this world, in myself? How can I learn to love this nervous system that makes me so small and in need of hiding? How do I, like some cancer patients, turn toward their tumor with mercy and actually send love into their disease? How do they do it? How much love does it take to accept, without force, illness into the heart of healing? How can I offer myself the kindness that flowed so effortlessly toward others? How do I overcome being hardwired to jumble words and meanings? How will anyone ever be able to understand me? How will I ever be loved?

I could do all the "mirror yoga" I was able to stay awake for—seeing myself as a loving other might, even trying to see myself as God might—but the danger of a thunderous judgment made me tremble a little bit. I started to practice simply seeing myself as being, not being someone who was OK sometimes, but rather just looking into simple beingness. Not so much personality, not someone, but maybe Oneness or something like the root without forcing the flower. Actually liberated!

It took years to let go of the idea of how different, and thus unacceptable, I was and to see myself as a heart in process. The heart's process was clearly to be of service to others. And in others I found more of myself. More to encourage, more to love. Eventually that nagging self-judgment morphed into the usual, mechanical, almost impersonal, "not enoughness" which needed watching. Meditation held me like I was its only child.

I still notice the old afflictive thoughts wishing I didn't have this wobbly brain, this unreliable nervous system, but with service to others and practice on myself, my heart opens again and again and I find comfort in what is.

TWO

Seeing and Hearing

By junior high school I knew that some people called me a "dirty Jew," but I didn't really know what a "Jew" was. My family never went to temple or celebrated any of the holidays in our home. My mother was a Jewish atheist. My father didn't "talk about such things." We were one of only four Jewish families in the town. The only other Jew I knew was the son of one of the families. When I was ten and he was sixteen, he tried to get me to touch his penis. Who were these people?!

Everyone else in my classes was Catholic. A few called me "Christ killer." I was frightened enough as it was without being a killer of someone they loved. Some of the tough girls would jeer anti-Semitic statements at me. One day, one of them pushed against the metal door of the bathroom stall just as I was getting up to leave and cracked me in the head hard enough to almost knock me out. Jews must have been pretty bad people, I thought.

I couldn't think of why they would be so angry at me. What had I ever done to hurt them? Why was I a "dirty Jew"? I didn't know anyone who wanted to kill the "son of God." I never wanted to harm anyone. I just wanted to be "in" so people would like me.

I thought maybe I should change my religion so I would be forgiven. I visited many types of Christian churches and eventually went to see a priest and asked him to teach me about being a Catholic. I took lessons for a year.

Prayer was very natural to me, and to be alone with God seemed ideal. I did the Serenity Prayer every morning:

Please grant me the serenity to accept the things I cannot change, the courage to change the things I can, and the wisdom to know the difference.

I spoke to Jesus nightly and asked forgiveness for anything I might have done. I didn't know what else to do. I promised God I would be the best Catholic He ever saw. I was a "good girl," I wasn't sexual, and I did not lie or steal as many of my peers did.

By the age of twelve, I was praying and reading everything I could find about God. I read the Bible to be a better Christian, but it was hard to understand. And when I asked the priest some questions, he said if I didn't understand I just had to have faith. But where was this faith I was supposed to automatically have? Was it because I had been a Jew that I was somehow cursed to be without it?

When I found out that Jesus had been a Jew, it floored me. How could being a Jew be such a bad, even unredeemable, thing? If he made it out of that, why couldn't I?

I asked God to forgive me, to love me.

People said I was a nonbeliever, but that was not what I felt. I was just confused about some things the priest said. Were people really set on fire for as long as eternity because they swore or didn't eat fish on Friday? Or worse, for just being born a Jew? Did that make sweet Jesus hate me?

I tried so long to be perfect but felt I had fallen far short of the mark. I was the proverbial lamb lost in the wilderness. I thought maybe I would be struck by lightning or something like that, so I turned to the One they said I had killed and asked for his forgiveness. But to my amazement instead of being punished for my confusion and lack of faith, Jesus, the God of Love, spoke in me, "You don't need to be different to be perfect."

Just beneath the surface I held a sacred essence close to my heart. Something I could not describe. I was praying my chest would break open and allow me in. I didn't know what it was, but I knew it was the only thing worth finding, what the Sufis later told me was the only secret worth knowing, "The Open Secret," deeper than my fear.

I knew this was what I was born for. I had more than just faith in God, I had trust. So I wasn't afraid to share my doubt and fear with this love I felt. I asked how there could be a benevolent God when there was so much suffering and pain. How could my father have been so hurt and my mother so wounded they could not hold me in their heart? How could my eleven-year-old neighbor get raped? How could there be so much injustice in the world? How could I be called "Christ killer"?

Not knowing if there was an answer, I had asked the question of the ages that had turned even the pious away from their faith. Fearing I may indeed have gone too far and asked the wrong question, I almost stopped breathing, it seemed. Then in the surrendered silence, my breath reappeared, breathing itself in and out of the level of mind we call the heart. In my heart love, I heard, "There is no benevolent God! Benevolence is a quality of the most human of hearts and one that a suffering world calls to action. Mercy is not up to God, it is up to you!"

Alone in my room, what was at first an abandonment slowly became monastic. At first I was wracked with loneliness, but gradually the aloneness became an "at-one-ment." My heart was my laboratory testing how lousy I could feel and still feel love. The love of some invisible creature who lived in the underground passage way between fear and love.

I prayed every day and every day learned what prayer was about. I found prayer in my first morning breath and wished only to hear my true heart in every breath that followed. Prayer expressed my heart.

At first my prayer beseeched the divine. I was praying to be a better, kinder person. After a long while, my prayers began to include the possibility of the well-being of others, sending increasing waves of loving kindness, a glimmer of forgiveness for myself and others, out into the world.

Prayer was instructing me how to pray with a bit less attachment and a deeper sort of listening.

Alone in my room with God, I never felt quite so lonely again.

One day my parents, going on a trip, dropped me off for a week with a family I had never met. I was met at the door by a friendly woman who invited me in. She greeted me warmly and introduced me to her five children, who were also friendly and quickly included me in their play. It was, I believe, a rather poor family who were probably watching me for whatever money my parents had offered them.

One of the most comforting things about this household was suppertime. The whole family ate together every night, which was an unusual experience for me, as our family ate together only on Thanksgiving and perhaps on Christmas. I liked how this family related to each other at the table. They actually exchanged the highlights of their day, looked at each other with true concern, and really listened. There were no dirty looks, no squinty eyes, no set jaw, no mental fists. No one was wishing they were somewhere else.

Generous in their play, the kids immediately included me in, but not, of course, without an initiation. Trying to scare me a little, they told me about "a creepy old man down the street" who lived alone in this huge, old Victorian house. They dared me to go knock on the door. But something in me sensed it might not have been quite as dangerous as my new acquaintances tried to make me believe. Perhaps, because I lived an isolated lifestyle, I cultivated a certain toughness as part of a necessary armor. I was always fond of old people, so calling the kids' bluff, I bravely climbed the broad stairs and knocked on the big door.

The old man opened the door, smiled at this brave little stranger, and invited me in. He had a friendly face and kind eyes. I entered with no hesitation. We had Kool-Aid and cookies.

He turned out to be one of the kindest men I had ever met. We played tic-tac-toe, a game I was unfamiliar with, for an hour. Handing me another glass of Kool-Aid, he told me about a big ballroom on the top floor of the house where he used to dance for hours with his wife and invited me up for a dance. It was the biggest house I had ever been in and, of course, since I loved to dance, I said yes. The ballroom was the full length of the home. It had wooden floors and floor-to-ceiling mirrors. Marvelous! He told me his wife loved to dance and that she was a dance teacher many years ago. He was very lonely. He had an old crank Victrola. He taught me the waltz and we waltzed together for a lovely long time.

After a while I thought I'd better get back to the kids, who probably wondered if I had been eaten by the old man or something. I said my good-byes, and he thanked me for being his friend. I told him I hoped to come back and see him some time, but as it turned out I never did. I never saw him again, but I think he was a contributing factor, along with my aunt, that inspired me later to study gerontology in college. And perhaps this is why my first form of service was in a local nursing home.

Seeing and Hearing

I think one of the reasons I felt ostracized by the "real world" was because I could "see" beyond it. The world seemed, as long as I can remember, to be melting at the edges. And I could "hear" at times what seemed another level of what minds said. I was often aware of the thoughts of others, which at times were quite disconcerting. So often this "hearing" of thoughts did not match what people were saying. It was confusing.

Sometimes I thought I was just plain crazy. The "hearing" was confirmed on occasion when I would ask someone, before they spoke, what they were thinking or what was on their mind. Sometimes I blurted out what I felt they were thinking and saw a fearful expression on their face. I learned not to do that too much.

Sleep became my best friend. And my dream life far exceeded my waking experience. Someone gave me a book on astral travel. "Oh, I know this stuff," my mind said. I experimented with getting the spirit to leave the body and go window-shopping elsewhere. This, in some ways, did not seem much of a challenge, as I was barely in my body as it was. My dreams became more interesting. But my heart still longed for a simpler place of rest.

I did a wakeful, sleeping practice every night for years. Then I thought I would try it on a boyfriend who I felt was fooling around. And it worked. I "saw" him in another part of town, with another girl. So when I returned from my astral travel, I got in my car and drove over to where I had seen him. The expression on his face was shock, to say the least. Of course, he thought it was just an unfortunate coincidence and fumbled out a few tepid excuses. The second time I caught him, he almost collapsed, and I could see him contemplating making a run for it.

I impressed a few people by casually mentioning where they had been and what they were up to the night before. Nowadays this would be called "bad juju," misuse of gifts given or called on. As if I wasn't already weird enough in their eyes! I thought if I showed some "power" that people would like me. Wrong state, wrong time; not California, not the '60s. I could always get their attention but I could never keep them in my life.

And just to add to the peculiarities of extrasensory mechanisms, there also arose what is called "distant seeing," considered a by-product, a "gift bag," from the Astral Projection Travel Service, whose most precious "gift" may be an ongoing questioning of perception itself. I was trying to separate the dream of consciousness from the reality of awareness.

I was trying to wake up, to awaken! I felt like I was getting vulcanized by God. All of which provided a feeling of power, as well as a vague sense of lunacy.

Also, of course, since nothing is more difficult to deal with than the impossible, I was somewhat relieved when I found out my picking up on others' thoughts was part of what is referred to in Transpersonal Psychological circles as "distant hearing." This seeming parlor trick, though of questionable value to all but the overweening ego, did become quite useful when I began working as an aide in hospitals and nursing homes, with people in coma and those that could barely speak.

Trusting the mystery, I listened and they "spoke" and we joined in something akin to therapy in the stillness of the ambient hospital symphony. I spoke to them about being kind to themselves, forgiving themselves, and speaking through their heart to those who may need forgiveness. I was also, of course, talking to myself through them.

A Word of Caution

This talk of astral travel and distant hearing and seeing may seem all too interesting, which is exactly what it is. These experiences are a major enticement for the ego and can become all too seductive for the cold and empty deeply unhealed place within us. They are a potential distraction from liberation.

After a while I said to myself, "I can't do this wobbly-pivot game anymore." I had been looking for powers to compensate for my feelings of social powerlessness, my feelings of frailty and vulnerability. I needed to be free even of these seeming strengths that just dug my misery even deeper.

These unusual abilities can easily become our isolating reaction to powerlessness. I had to stop trying to cultivate reactionary defenses against the truth that none of all this made me any more loving or any more forgiving. These energies did not make me special but only more separate, only more different. Only less connected. How were they serving anyone? How were they deepening the self-mercy and forgiveness we all need?

Many of these so-called gifts do more to impress others than clear the way to the heart. In fact some such gifts can actually turn out to be traps, trapping us in the sticky ego just short of the real purpose we took birth for.

As I write about all this now, if you asked me to display these gifts, I would not be able to do it. After using this talent for three years to perfect what came to be seen by me as parlor tricks in this context, capable of attracting attention, but incapable of giving me anything worth holding to, I thanked the giver but returned the gifts. Of all these seeming gifts, all these glimpses of the Mystery in a minor key, the greatest gift was the ability to let go.

More Gifts

Even though I still had to move a straight edge (usually a ruler) down the page to keep the words from twisting and flying around, I loved books. And bookstores. The Existentialists, Gurdjieff, Ouspensky, and Alan Watts changed my life before my very eyes. I read *Siddhartha* and all else I could find by Hesse. I read *The Aquarian Gospel*, and what I understood of Zen and the mysticism of Jesus fit right in.

I was deeply moved by these writings. They freed in me something I could barely describe. I think it was the heart. Though I still had no one to speak with about these insights, I nonetheless heard myself say, "a-hah!" aloud during many of these readings. I watched my small mind expanding daily.

As a way to deal with my changing life, I began what became long periods of a half-mystical state of sleep and particularly lucid dreaming. To set the backdrop for whatever question I might have in mind, just before falling asleep, I would envision what I wanted to dream about.

My dream life was quite wonderful at times, filled with a love and play my usually isolated self was unfamiliar with. It was the start of a whole new life, my next incarnation. Some shadows of the punishing God continued to interrupt my life, but it was easier to hold my confusion about God in this growing heart than it was to redirect it to the old pathways—the guilt, shame, and fear that I had hoped God would shield me from.

Naturally, my practice fluctuated between self and other. Between what I was clinging to for myself and what freedom from that same restriction I wished for others. I was disappointed when looking deeper. Where I expected to find faith, there was doubt. Where there should have been love, there was selfishness. Where perhaps generosity might have been, there was greed. I could feel myself struggling to be free. Pulling me close then pushing myself away. Still entangled in the snares of "fear and loathing," of the habitual cycle of liking and disliking myself and everything I came in contact with, even in the mind. My rudder was not steady, but at least I had my hands on the tiller.

Blessedly, in a world separated by violence, there also came to my attention a large colorful image of the Hindu God of Love as baby Krishna, Jesus in the arms of the Mother, the children of the Peaceable Kingdom, the lion lying down with the lamb. In the divine outreach of compassion, of kindness, of one creature for another, I knew what I was looking for, the thought of which quickened my heart.

"Until the fever broke
and my heart could not abide a moment longer,
as the rest of me awoke, summoned from the dream,
not half caring for anything but love."

THREE

Lifting the Brain Veil

BEFORE I WAS INFORMED that I was "profoundly dyslexic," I just thought I was stupid and too weird to cultivate friends. I often talked too much, or not at all. In school, I would get an A for creativity over a D for atrocious grammar—"excellent creative thinking," the teacher said, "but nearly untranslatable into English." I was having considerable difficulty reading anything, much less a map. I had trouble telling my right from my left, I could not comprehend most directions, I was lost much of the time. Infrequently, I was given to a rather loud swearing when startled at a time and in places where such behavior was taboo. I was like an acrobat falling from tightrope to tightrope, never quite able to find a natural balance.

I often counted numbers to myself to get my grounding. The counting, quite unexpectedly, began to intensify my concentration, which brought some calm to the twisty mind. Though it originated from a sense of weakness, it gave me some strength and steadiness. It was manna from heaven for a wobbly dyslexic.

I had, for much of my life, difficulty with the waves and troughs of my speech patterns. I had not yet found the middle way. It made communication and connections quite uncomfortable and added a compulsive repetitiveness. I constantly attempted to say things clearer. I often immediately forgot what people said because my memory files opened and closed so rapidly. I heard myself speaking out loud what I imagined I was just thinking. It was a mess. I left out my nouns and sometimes verbs when I was speaking. People shook their heads in confusion. I certainly wasn't going to go out for the debate team, much less keep a friend for very long.

But I had, perhaps, some gifts in the midst of this whirlwind of confusion. I had an excellent long-term memory. Though I may not have known where I was, I knew well where I had been. Through visualization I learned to take a mental picture of a page, for instance, and refer back to it verbatim when asked a question.

My brain just isn't wired the same as that of most people. I see life in pictures. That is why it was so difficult to find the right words quickly enough to communicate well. I have to riffle through a number of images before I can tune into what is an appropriate response. I understand much more easily if I see a photo or if someone draws a picture of what they mean. I can read a sentence and have high comprehension but an inability to repeat the words, almost a kind of paralysis, when I attempt such a task.

When someone speaks, I have to find the corresponding files and access them, which takes time to figure out what they really mean since I think very literally. I put these pictures together to come up with ideas of what to say and how to say it. Sometimes I also experienced a symptomatic echoing when people spoke, finding myself in an echo chamber where speech bounced back and forth so rapidly I had difficulty recalling what was being said. Often people must have thought I was not paying attention because the echo often erased the last fragment.

Because this process is slower than conversation, it makes me nervous or anxious, and I often don't say exactly what I mean the first time and have to repeat myself to be clear, which makes others nervous as well.

Animals also think in images rather than words, which could be why throughout my life I have had an extraordinary draw toward animals. I think I would have been more balanced and happy if I had gone to college to be a veterinarian.

I was poor at reading people's true intentions because I often didn't interpret facial expressions well and watched their mouths more often than their eyes. Luckily, because of the sensitivity of the intuition I had developed by watching my silent parents' body language, I was able to understand more of what was going on.

This anxiety is caused by an automatic overload of the amygdala region of the brain, which functions in response to stress with a "fight or flight" reaction, a "high alert" flooding the system with adrenalin. This experience only serves to amplify feelings of tension, lack of safety, and considerable discomfort. In my case, because of the biological malfunction I was born with, I stayed on high alert longer than required. In time this can be somewhat, if not greatly, mollified by the grounding action of mindfulness and heartfulness practices.

Getting into concentration exercises helped me evolve from *reacting* to old fears and anxieties to *responding* to them. This even extended into my dreams, as I was learning to respond to the content of the passing show of images and thoughts rather than give in to that old urge to withdraw and even hide from the mind. I was becoming less compulsively reactive.

I learned to soften my body and watch my states of mind with a bit more compassion for myself. My life was no longer an emergency.

At times I still have anxiety about the workings of my brain, but if afflictive emotions get too seductive and threaten to pull me down under the waves, I release my pushing and pulling at such thoughts and instead begin to relate to them directly on the level of sensation. Not burying the thoughts, but letting them go on as they will and continuing to relate to them as sensations moving through the body. Not clinging or condemning the passing show of mind, but watching it as the comings and goings of the dance of life in the field of sensation.

Different Ways of Seeing Dyslexia

When I was young, I often dreamed of being a Native American. Most of the dreams were mundane, viewing scenes from the outside. But a few, the most memorable, were experienced from the inside. I was a person in that life. These dreams confused me because I never read any Native American books or had an interest in their culture.

One dream has stayed with me for years. I was, it seems, a shaman, a healer. I was dying. I was lying on the soft grassy ground just watching the people around me. Mothers and children were playing, fathers were cutting wood and skinning animals. Life seemed peaceful and good. People seemed healthy and happy. A few friends came over to where I was lying and asked me how I was feeling. I told them I felt like life was passing out of me.

I was a *Heyoka*, a man highly prized, a tribal oddity, a social outsider who often hung out with the women, not with warriors but healers, known for doing things backward, riding backward, eating with the opposite hand, saying yes for no, etc. My dream body did everything backward, or in an unusual manner. It spoke in a scrambled, even reverse way. I now think this archetype could be the predecessor of those born dyslexic.

With my friends gathered around me, I started to fall asleep. I could feel them try to pick me up and bring me inside. I felt like I weighed a thousand pounds but couldn't speak to them. They called over more men, and although there were eight of them, they could not move me an inch. They sat with me and chanted and sang for a long time, praying. I felt at peace and watched my mind looking back over my life with some joy and some sadness.

This experience went on for many hours. It was timeless. I could see the day end and begin again. I saw the mind as a personality, but

I was not that personality. I was pure *amness*, undifferentiated being. I felt like light moving through timelessness. I was just dying. My fellow tribesmen brought over my family to say good-bye. Others too came to say how much I had helped them, but I didn't pay attention to their words. I only paid attention to my passing energy. I was completely at peace.

It was one of those real dreams, the kind which remains for years. I didn't know what it meant, but I knew it was true.

Some years later I found a book called *Smart but Feeling Dumb* that helped me understand something of the workings of a brain that finds it difficult to learn in the "normal" manner. The author, Harold Levinson, had two dyslexic daughters and surmised it was an inner ear/cerebellum and eye disorder. He spoke about many styles of dyslexia including a social dysmorphia, making me look in the mirror like a homely horse face looking back, making things bob and float while I tried to connect with people, a kind of social dyslexia that kept my feet from quite touching the ground. Some dyslexics can't read, others can't spell. Many visualize, taking mental photos of whatever they need to read. Others memorize words but still have trouble correctly sounding them out. I had all of the above. I still can't sound out words well no matter how much I break them into syllables.

Levinson helped me understand what was going on inside me. He gave me great confidence when he wrote it was my brain, not my mind that needed tilting. He made me laugh just when I needed it.

He showed me I wasn't stupid, but actually a jigsaw puzzle master who had taught myself to piece together what was being seen and heard, and then to fit it together in a recognizable manner. If my grade school teachers had told me this, it might have saved me incarnations of shame and confusion.

I never met another dyslexic person until I met the well-known physician/healer/writer Gerald Jampolsky, the fellow who started the centers for Attitudinal Healing. He didn't find out he was dyslexic until his second year of medical school. What a beautiful person he is. Sometimes I wonder if having undiagnosed learning disabilities doesn't separate the heart from the mind and leave even some of the smartest people feeling lost and irretrievable.

Calming the Mind

When I started my first practice, *mantra*, I learned to steady myself and watch how the intentional repetition of a phrase began to quiet down the unintentional, compulsive repetitions of my mind. The practice provided me spaces between thoughts from which to simply watch and slow the habitual tendency to react rather than respond. As time went on and I learned to meditate, I was able to see what was going on in the passing show on the screen of consciousness. I saw I didn't have to jump at every stimulus and could let what was superfluous just sail by, which naturally lessened the anxiety in my interactions.

Anxiety and fear arise with neurological disorders, but this doesn't mean that you are "a dysfunctional being." It just means you have specific work to do on yourself that will help you adjust to your surroundings.

It's all too easy to slap labels on ourselves, to judge ourselves to be outsiders unfit for normal society. (Not that being an outsider is a bad thing when that becomes a conscious choice to move beyond the chatter and clatter of the common milieu.) Most conditions are at least somewhat workable with a patient cultivation of concentration and a nonjudgmental effort to liberate oneself.

In saying, "Judge not, lest you be judged," Jesus was slipping a rare secret under our cell door, revealing that the nature of the judging-mind doesn't know us from the person next to us and treats all with equal mercilessness.

It takes awhile to calm the mind and allow the heart to feel safe, to come into its own, like coming to the surface, but who has anything better to do?

When I started living with Stephen, the pain was diminishing as I came to see with considerable relief that my dreaded word scramble small talk was a conduit for the heart, actually a means of communicating love. The tension of resistance to boredom and self-righteousness responded to the hardening and softening of the belly and the letting go of separation. Kind of a "hold and release" experience where we find ourselves lost and let go, calling ourselves home. My long-conditioned speech patterns softened as love became the primary means of communication. Acceptance bonds.

My awareness practices changed much of this in a most wonderful manner. Of course, I still have the personality I was dealt, with all the twists and turns of organic brain issues, but practice has given me the insight and method to relate "to" states of mind and not "from" them. I often experience myself watching "anxiety" now rather than just being "anxious."

I am considerably freer than in my youth, with more room to live in and, thankfully, greater access to my heart. I think people who in my youth once shunned me as weird might now just find me a bit eccentric.

The Flowering of the Heart

I always feared that I might get so far away from my heart that I would never find my way back. That quote from Dante's *Inferno* which says, "Abandon all hope, ye who enter here," gave me a chill.

In time, of course, I came to see that this saying was a blessing, not a curse. That "hope" has as many levels as does the mind and is often based on fear and a sense of helplessness. Investigating and letting go of the fear that masqueraded as hope and held me back from fruition brought a new confidence to my process and a greater trust in taking my next unknown step. It was a blessing capable of turning hell to heaven and helping me go to the edge of the living truth, where all growth occurs.

As I mentioned earlier, I started working at a local hospital and nursing home with patients others did not care to attend to. The elderly patients who were so sick and so alone were lined up each morning against the walls in the hallways, longing to be touched, longing for someone who somehow reminded them of a long-lost loved one. The appreciation I got from them gave me a sense of being able to help, to do some good as perhaps nowhere else. My heart discovered the hope that borders on faith and trust that seamlessly enters the future with an answer that brings us all back into the human race.

It turned out that those in a coma were not "gone" but just hanging out on the mezzanine. They were not on the second floor, but just watching from above, so to speak. It is difficult for me to find the right language to describe this, but a few of the people who recovered from their comas would occasionally, with considerable gratitude, thank me for my support "while we were together in there."

An example of the ability to tune into another's breath and perhaps sense their thoughts while in coma occurred at a Conscious Living/Conscious Dying workshop while Stephen and I were relating some of our experiences bedside with comatose patients, when a local physicist approached us and begged us to see his wife in a coma in a nursing home a few blocks away. The event was near a major research center, and some of the participants were scientists who were obviously skeptical of what they thought of as our "woo" science. The physicist who approached us was breaking a taboo by looking behind the mind to find a deeper truth, but his wife had been in a coma for three months and if we could just visit her for a few minutes, he would be eternally grateful. So we did, entering her room lightly, saying hello, we introduced ourselves while positioning ourselves on either side of the bed. She had, he said, been in a completely comatose state since Christmas Eve.

Almost at once, Stephen and I picked up her state of mind. She was extremely angry! And it was not just as a reaction to her condition.

After a few minutes by her side, we excused ourselves and asked her husband if we might talk to him out in the hallway. We asked if there was something else going on between them that might be so upsetting to her. He was very surprised at the question. His body stiffening, he blanched, and after a moment began to stutter that he was having an affair with her nurse. He broke down crying, beside himself with shame and fear. He said he was a good Catholic and couldn't understand how he had allowed this to happen! And how on earth could she know? What could he do now? He had felt, seeing her lying there inert in a coma, as if she was already dead, but he was wrong and causing her a lot of unintended pain.

We suggested that he and his wife's nurse speak to his comatose wife, admit to the affair, and ask for her forgiveness. We suggested he spend a little time relating how very lonely and confused he had been, how their relationship had been souring for some time, and how sympathetic and consoling the kind and attractive nurse had been. And then that the nurse, too, should go in alone and speak to his wife, telling her how very how sorry she was for causing her pain.

The nurse called us some days later to report that they had, awkwardly at first, but then feeling the appropriateness of it, "told her everything." After a couple of days there was a noticeable relaxing of his wife's countenance, what seemed to be a releasing of subliminal tension. And changes in many noticeable markers were observed by several of the staff.

A few weeks later he called to say he had gone to see her daily, speaking to her as if across the breakfast table, and feeling that perhaps they had resolved some long unfinished business between them. Soon after, she died in what appeared to be considerable peace, her husband and the children lovingly by her side.

Like many, I left my parents' home looking for my true family, the family that trusts and supports the heart's work and remains present for the mind's travail. I needed to learn how to touch, how to feel, and how to laugh and play. Most certainly I needed to connect with others, if not to be loved as I wished, then certainly to love and offer what I could that served others—whatever was of use from what I called my weirdness.

Later on when Stephen and I led healing groups, we would ask how many felt they were born into their true family, a family which accepted them "as is." Less than half would raise their hands. But it is often hard to recognize, because we are so close to the confusion, the value of the pain that broke our heart and opened it to others.

I now thank my parents, from a distance, for the isolating silence that helped to sharpen my inner senses. It was "the gift in the wound." The gift of healing that grows in the heart of every injury, the shared pain that can attune one heart to another, that can convert being alone with "my pain" to being at one with "the pain" in another, which heals all involved.

I think being raised in a house of silence may have helped to develop my "hearing." If I wanted to understand what was going on behind the family mask, I had to sharpen my focus and listen deeper. It was not so much a gift as a survival technique, one I was to learn would prove useful for working with people who were dying and needed to tie up some loose end or some sort of unfinished business that was gnawing at them even in the depth of coma.

FOUR

Call Waiting

AT SEVENTEEN, I FELL in love. It took two years, but when he bought and inscribed matching wedding bands, I felt I could brave hell and even have intercourse. I was confused and fearful that I might be making a huge mistake, but because he said we were getting married and because he was so insistent, I gave in. He was joining the army. I wore his wedding band, and he said we would get married as soon as he got back from Vietnam.

We had sex and it was nice but not at all what I thought it would be. I thought I should have felt some pain and bled, but nothing like that happened. What I mostly felt afterward was shame. And I prayed for forgiveness.

A few months later when he got out of boot camp, I decided to surprise my boyfriend. I used my last dollar and took a bus to where he was staying in Ohio so we might get married. I got a hotel room and called him and left a message. He came over, we made love, and he immediately left. It felt very strange! I called him many times after that, but he never replied.

A few days after that, he had a friend come over to tell me our relationship was over. I was devastated. I had no money to get home so I decide to hitchhike, not caring whether I lived or died.

I never saw my boyfriend again. I heard rumors he got out of the military after a year in Vietnam and told everyone I was a whore for having sex with him. I was at a loss and depressed; I felt so confused.

I went to a fellow I had known for many years and asked if I could confide in him. He said he was "open to listening." While we were talking, he brought out some sort of cigarette. I had never smoked, but he told me to try this, this was different than tobacco and might make me feel better. I tried it and got very high. I had never felt like this before. He started to kiss me and we began to have sex. I was barely there. Unlike the first time, I felt a lot of pressure, it hurt a little, and a lot of blood ran down my leg. I was so embarrassed. I didn't know what was wrong.

In an ironic flash, I realized that I had still been a virgin, that my first boyfriend never broke my hymen. (Maybe he just wasn't willing to commit.) Then I thought, "I am really in trouble with God now!" I thought God had given me a second chance and I blew it. I thought I would burn in hell for sure because I let Him down. I needed penance, some kind of special dispensation if I was going to get through this one!

Sometimes I thought my love for Jesus was going to be the only love I would ever know. I never heard the word "love" used in our house. Out in the world I only heard "love" associated with possessions: things that people owned and lost. They loved their new car, their new shoes, and their boyfriend's football jacket. But I didn't want the possessive love that took instead of gave. I wanted the love that possessed me, that helped me discover who I really was beneath the numbness, that opened my heart and brought me back to life. Love was my precious secret.

Sometimes when I look back and recount my difficult early life, it is tough to distinguish between compassion for myself and good old self-pity. Perhaps, it was being so alone with my feelings that encouraged me to have empathy for others, the catalyst that led me to begin working with the sick and dying. My isolation gave me permission to resonate with the predicaments of others, and it guided my heart through the grief and love we all share. This increasing empathy was the voice of the spirit coming to the surface.

I had pushed away so many parts of myself that I found it difficult to discover who I was underneath all the hiding and resistance.

To open to myself with kindness and healing is the merciful healing I took birth for.

Working with others, I found I no longer needed to manipulate myself toward a superficial happiness that blocked the depth of my true feelings in order to be whole. I learned to take myself into my heart, "as is." And, in so doing, I was able to love another wholeheartedly, just as I was able to accept their love. When we open to our life, sometimes emotions can be explosive and make us sweat with fear. Part of my healing was to let my pain come into our family taboo—the heart.

Decades later, when Stephen and I were first teaching together at one of his long-established grief workshops, I heard someone say that as a child they had been "a model prisoner." I felt a chill run up my spine. That had been my survival mechanism as a child as well.

In the grief workshops we encouraged the freedom of self-expression. "You can't let go of anything you can't accept." Many, like myself, were there to complete something very old and to become something quite new. They came to free their life; to liberate their precious breath to serve the breath of others, no longer "keeping it all to themselves" as imposed by families and cultures afraid of appearing weak.

The freedom not to judge others for what we fear in ourselves was a brave new world for me to share with those I was just meeting but knew so well in my heart.

Where do we go when we can't show our feelings to our parents, siblings, or friends? Where do we go when we feel that if we show our feelings we will be destroyed? We often go to our pillows, which is where I learned to cry. We learn to smother our feelings and then feel smothered by life.

Part of my learning to cry included learning to scream, to break the safety valve and explode into being. Soon after I started finding myself, I came across the energetic release of "Primal Scream" work, which was quite helpful. When we hear someone scream, as we naturally turn to rescue them, the gift in the wound becomes evident. To our amazement, a wave of compassion for ourselves washes over us with a loving kindness we are yet to comprehend. Is this the love beyond comprehension that Jesus whispered of?

Dancing in a Cage

At nineteen, having practiced dance for so long, I decided to make it my job. I mustered my courage and went to one of the local clubs to ask for a job. I started an independent life, dancing in a strobe-lit go-go cage, wearing little white boots, black fish-net stockings, short shorts, and a sparkling sequin top. I worked days as an aide in the hospital, intermittently going to night school, and for two years also danced at night in the club. I danced my loneliness and feelings of abandonment away before a libidinous sea of half-drunk men.

It was odd for someone who was hardly in her body. I was the "weirdly helpful girl in white" during the day and the babe in boots and sequins dancing in the go-go cage at night. Schizophrenic, you say?! Maybe so. But in this weirdness I found a much needed self-regard that reinforced my ability to listen, to hear from the shared heart.

The ornamental cage was, of course, no protection against my fear of all the leering drunks. After a few followed me back to my rented room, I bought a gun. When one man staggered up against my door and tried to push his way in, I stuck my gun in his face and neither he nor anyone else at the bar ever followed me home again. Soon, though, because I didn't like the way a gun felt in my hands, I threw it in the river.

Much to my shock, my parents showed up one night. They were clearly disturbed, and it was the first time I ever saw them drink alcohol. They left quickly.

So after my parents ran out, one of the gangster-owners, in a bizarre attempt to console me, took out a large roll of cash and offered me $3,000 if I would have sex with a favorite customer. I said, why not, thinking this would get me out of debt—after all, it was only sex. I agreed to meet the guy at a hotel room. I went there and waited for him. I was nervous and scared of what he might want me to do. It was something I hadn't given much thought to before that moment. Oops!

When the cigar smoking, well-dressed, fiftyish guy walked into the room, I knew in an instant this scene was not for me. I felt sorry for the guy and, politely excusing myself, I headed for the elevators.

It was time to make a big change, and I thought that if I married my musician boyfriend at the time, I could start a wholesome new life. I had met this guy when I was twenty. He played saxophone for the opening band when I danced with Curtis Mayfield's *The Drifters*. I got pregnant the first time we were together. I didn't want to get married, but for the child's sake, we did. He was traveling with his band when I went into early labor. I was having a lot of bleeding and went to the hospital alone.

When my hand touched the hospital door, I had the distinct feeling (karmic recall?) that I had made a terrible mistake. I heard a voice say, "You weren't going to do this and now look at what you have done!" Yet it was my son's birth that did so much to open my heart.

The doctor said I was having a placenta previa. I was six weeks early. As I went into a very difficult labor, I felt like I was being ripped apart. I writhed and rocked back and forth but didn't make a sound. I cried silently. I had had a lot of practice for keeping silent in pain. I heard the nurse say, "She's ready." They rolled me into the birthing room and put a mask over my face. The next thing I knew it was three hours later and I had given birth. They told me I had a baby boy. I was overjoyed and named him James.

The next day I tried to get up, but the pain kept me down. I had several dozen stitches inside and out. Later, I was told I should have had a C-section. My husband was still on the road, so after a ten-day stay in the hospital, I went to my parents' home to wait for his return.

After only a month in my parents' home, the contagion of their stress made me realize that there was no time like the present to give birth to myself and get free of this long sadness. They didn't want any babies in their quiet home. I didn't want their shrieking silence to make my son feel as unwelcome as I had felt.

My husband stopped by for a day, then disappeared again. I went to his mother's home, which was a good deal more hospitable. She watched James while I went out to get a job and look for an apartment because my husband said he couldn't come up with the money to support us.

I tried traveling with the band for a while, spending four months in Hawaii in a third-rate boarding house. He was out cheating and often arrived home with the rising sun. It was a pretty unsavory place for a child or a depressed mother. There was no room for any of us to complete our birth.

As it turned out, I was divorced within two years. I asked my ex-husband to stay in touch with his beautiful son, to even just send him a card or call once in a while. But he never has.

Birth Day

My ex-husband left me with a beautiful baby boy and a considerable disappointment with the institution of marriage. Confused is hardly the word for what I felt!

I never realized how difficult it would be to work fifty-plus hours a week and give James the care I knew he needed. I had never been so sleep-deprived before or felt quite so isolated or alone, a stranger in a strange land, with no one to talk to about my baby's needs or my own.

It was so difficult for me to relate to James that I felt nearly catatonic. I hardly knew how to respond to myself, so I didn't have a clue how to mother anyone else. I read book after book about bringing up children, but without role models, I didn't know how to apply any of what I read. I'm sure I confused my poor son. I had so little heart available. How to be playful was foreign to me.

Like many premature babies, James had colic and cried day and night. I felt I was a terrible mother. How could I help him? How could I stop his crying? I feared that maybe he, as I had in my youth, thought he had gotten off at the wrong stop. Medical people assured me premature babies often exhibit this sort of visceral discomfort.

I used a rocking chair and tried music, but nothing really helped. He was constipated and I had to give him suppositories every day to ease his stomach pains. I took him to two more doctors who said they had no medicine for him.

I was alone and desperate, going crazy for almost a year, until finally something in the "mothering gene" I was certain I did not possess intuited that he must have been allergic to the formula and milk. I stopped the milk and fed him more from my plate, and it seemed he settled more into his body. He still had some cramps, but it turned out the poor little guy had a double hernia and needed an operation.

I went on welfare to help pay for the operation, but the government agency refused me, so I picketed their office for a week until they finally gave him the operation he needed. He never had a stomach ache again.

James was a quiet, undemanding child, so I often missed some of the cues he sent out. It has always seemed evident that the place I most missed the mark ("missing the mark" being Alan Watt's definition of something like, or adjacent to, the misnomer of "sin") was with James's early raising. After all my accusations of my parents' inattentiveness and wounded silence, I made some of the same mistakes. It wasn't that I turned away from James as I felt my parents had done with me in my childhood. We went to children's shows and other events, I read many books on child psychology from Bettelheim and others, but I was slow to recognize his needs. It seemed I was a little lacking in the appropriate legacy of child care.

Feeling My Way

I sought counseling but could only afford two sessions. At the time, I was completely unaware of the clinics available to those with limited funds. I saved for a few months to get enough money to go to a counseling session. The talk helped me unload but had no practical application to help me deal with the depression or to know how to be more loving.

By this time I had twice tried, halfheartedly, to kill myself. The first time I tried to drown myself, but someone saved me. The second time I hit myself in the head with a rock, but it was too painful and didn't work either. I didn't know what to do. So many of the "weird experiences" that I later found to be gifts I felt at the time were signs of going mad.

I was deeply depressed and after about a year signed myself into a mental institution. My therapist blinded me with thorazine so that for the first two hours of the day all I saw was colors, no forms, and I had to feel my way along the wall to get to the bathroom. My therapist was like a bobble doll just nodding her head, "yes," "no." She never looked me in the eye.

The institute didn't hold much interest for me or help me chip away at any of the wall I had secreted myself within, so I signed myself back out after a little more than a month.

I met some beautiful people in the institution. They drew on a nurturing compassion waiting in my aching heart. I felt a lot of love. Some were gay and had been hidden away to be "cured," not to embarrass their wealthy families. Some only had eating problems. Some wanted a divorce and were put away until they changed their minds.

Some of these people who were put away because they saw auras or heard voices, I now realize, could have made a good living in California. I never met anyone really crazy by my terms. What they needed was exactly what they were being deprived of: mercy and a touch of familial love.

When I got out of the institution, I held my baby closer, cut my hair, got an Afro, and moved into a very warm-hearted communal house (one of those huge Victorians so plentiful in New England). I worked cleaning houses, took care of my boy with help from my housemates, and went to school at night.

After signing myself out of the mental institute, I tried many processes to heal my mind and heart. I went to a Fritz Perls's "Primal Scream Workshop" and then went home and gargled. I read and practiced as much as I could before the mirror of cognitive therapies, past life reviews, Wiccan thought, whatever insight might be found in astrology, and the traditional teachings of the *I Ching*—all in order to explain and soothe my pain. These practices were useful and sometimes uplifting. These great wisdom schools instilled a kindness toward myself and an inquisitive interest in the healing inherent in the mind and body. They reinforced my intention to heal, and gave me another language for what ailed me and a sense of where the healing might be found.

It was James who taught me how to be a better person as I learned to love by watching how unloving I could be. It broke my heart to see how much of this wonderful opportunity I had missed out on. But at a certain point the heart intercedes and reminds us to forgive, beginning with others, and finding our way back to ourselves. Observing how our intentions to be kind increase with the awareness of how much pain everyone seems to be in; how universal feelings of guilt, helplessness, hopelessness, and shame weakened our confidence in reconnecting with our wholeness.

When I could get just a single breath of mercy, of forgiveness, in a storm of self-condemnation, a bit of ground was cleared for something better to grow. Having mercy on myself was some of the hardest work I ever had to do.

When I could sit and listen to the still small voice within and just watch the living sensations that accompanied each breath, I was able to observe the mind settle down a bit. There seemed more room in my heart, more space to see even judgmental thoughts passing through.

On a rare day, I could momentarily see the emptiness, the space my thoughts were floating in; see the process of my thoughts, instead of just the difficult content; watch thought-by-thought my discontent; and begin to relate to my thoughts instead of react from them. It was a great relief!

AN ASIDE

As we write, I remind myself that it wasn't only me that needed to do this work on self-forgiveness. Stephen, as a youth, was a pretty bad guy. He was a heroin addict and a criminal. But he worked his way loose from his impulses and addictions and came out, after years of very hard work, as someone to admire. He still shudders at times for the harm he caused others.

Missing the signals of James's needs were my first lessons in self-forgiveness. I had been lost in myself instead of being there for him. Then I heard about an Indian teacher who was teaching a mantra to thousands of people who were apparently receiving considerable benefit. I thought, Why not try this one? I was desperate, and when the instructor, in a very formal setting, leaned over and whispered my personal mantra into my ear, I had high hopes. It sounded like "I'm." What was that I asked? just to be sure. He said, as if speaking for the Mystery itself, "No, the mantra cannot be said again!"

And I worked with "I'm" for a year. But I wondered, I'm what? I'm good? I'm bad? I simply am! (this was the best of the bunch), I'm here? I'm not here? Am I there or not? Where the hell am I?

It was judgmental torture, until a year later I found the word "OM" in a book about mantras. I laughed out loud. "No, No, Ondrea," my mind said, "Your mantra isn't 'I'm' it's 'OM!'" and OM settled into my nervous energy.

It was my study of the Asian teachings, Buddhist and Hindu, which seemed to resonate most deeply.

My Second Coming

My drive to find better and better places to live on almost no money further and further from cities and closer to nature repeatedly cut James off from much-wanted friends. He naturally resented this insensitivity on my part. Perhaps, still numb from my own youth, I was not sensitive to a young boy's emotional needs.

This was the beginning of a great lesson in caring for another and of learning how not to be the center of the universe and to love someone, something that needed more from me than I needed from them. It was my first experience of non-greedy love. It took me a long time to integrate all this into my small life. I had a lot to learn, but I was up to the task.

My work—doing house-cleaning yoga, vacuuming, and painting apartments—helped me save enough money to move out of the city to my beloved woods. I got an inexpensive apartment and a dog for James. In exchange for my rent, I vacuumed the apartments in the complex. It was a lot of work but I didn't need a babysitter, and I even babysat other children at night. To maintain a balance between the inside and the outside of my life, I read a lot and listened to music.

I still found it hard, though, to make friends, as I was difficult to understand, sometimes forgetting to put nouns in my sentences; and my verbs had a life of their own. People who didn't know me thought I either had a tumor or was mentally deficient. But I enjoyed the peace and quiet of a small town near the woods, the winding roads, and especially in autumn the wonderful meditative walks. I felt more peaceful than I had in years.

I still laugh at how much energy I put into the wrong mantra. Repeating the correct mantra while I vacuumed cleaned me and the rug at the same time with a considerable calming effect.

Then, one day, walking down the street, I had a rather unusual experience. All of a sudden I felt as if an enormous weight was lifted from me. I started to feel freer and happier than I could ever remember. I felt a vibrational energy entering and surrounding me. Golden atoms filled the air. Time stopped. My mind became uniquely clear. It was like a prayer come true. Something had fundamentally changed within me.

I was never the same again. I saw all living beings as connected energetically. Some might call this an experience of metaphysical insight, but at the time it just seemed an ordinary truth that had always been there but had gone unnoticed. This was my Second Coming!

I thought I had better not mention this experience to anyone, and I didn't until many years later when I moved to Taos and met Stephen, my spiritual partner. He said he too knew this territory, had known such moments of spaciousness, and reveled in having a partner able to traverse the "long and winding road" of self-discovery.

My going inward and finding Stephen standing beside me was the next step in my evolution. For some people such changes can turn their life upside-down. For me, it turned my life right-side-up. Or more accurately, it polished and clarified some of my old ways of seeing. It was a touch of grace, which reassured me of the presence of my original nature somewhere behind what I considered my far-flung mind.

Sensing a profound interconnectedness with life encouraged the feasibility of doing more service work. I became more available to people who were shut in because of illness, which led to the continuation of my counseling and working with dying patients as well as in nursing homes and as an aide in hospitals.

I focused on helping others, becoming known as someone available to those who were dying. I remember visiting a neighbor in the hospital. As I was leaving, I heard another patient crying in her room. I had heard her the day before when I was visiting my friend, so this time I went in and asked if I could be of any help. She had no visitors and could not speak English. I spoke no Spanish, but I sensed what she needed was deeper than language. I sat down in a chair next to her, reached out for her hand, and just sat there looking into her eyes. Her pain was palpable and she could see the tears in my eyes also. She kept saying "Ay Dios, Ay Dios" over and over and I knew what she meant. She was pleading for the end of her pain. I held her hand and let her know she was not alone, that her God said she was as deserving of love as anyone ever born, and she should see herself through her Dios's eyes. What she heard was not in my words, but from Dios in our heart-to-heart connection.

The next day I went into another room and found an emaciated old woman who had been left sitting for hours on a hard bed pan. She kept saying, "Why am I here? I just want to go home." Although there was little I could do directly, it seemed that just having someone who cared about her was strong medicine. I visited many people in that ward after that, and the nurses never asked me why I was there and even began to give me a little smile when we passed in the corridors.

Years later, when Stephen and I taught healing techniques in hospitals and visited patients under the guise of pastoral care, with official name tags and all, nothing was really different. It was the same hospital smells, the same tears, the same *Dios* beside us as some divine intuition guided us to offer our hearts into their open wounds.

And James turned out to have a quiet and patient nature, a quick sense of humor, much like Stephen's. He had an unusual combination of talents, which made him the state wrestling champion, and he displayed a skillful hand at art and a casual manner that made all at ease. These served him well as he continued an affinity with numbers, math in particular, providing him decades of employment and a well-respected seniority in his job at a casino. He grew up.

FIVE

Not the Body

WHEN I WAS TWENTY-EIGHT, it was discovered I had cancer.

It was discovered during the annual pap smear I was mandated by welfare to undergo in order to continue getting birth control pills. The lab results came back with an abnormal reading. After many more tests, I was told to go into the hospital for a cervical examination and a biopsy. I didn't think much of it and felt I probably had an infection. When my lab work came back, it was cancer! I was shocked and really scared. Cancer was a deadly loss of control.

I didn't connect it at the time, but it later struck me that this cancer occurred right where the doctor, the year before, had intentionally torn my cervix. He had been outspokenly prejudiced against women on welfare. I could feel that he was judging me when he told me my uterus needed to be straightened. He then proceeded to insert a long metal clamp all the way up to my cervix. Grasping and pulling sharply, he painfully tore my cervix, intentionally rendering me sterile.

I asked some friends if they ever had or heard of such a procedure or condition. No one had, nor had any of the gynecologists I spoke with. I should have filed a complaint, but I just wanted to get out of there.

A year later, a much kinder physician at the hospital where I had the biopsy told me that because of the cancer, my cervix had to be removed as soon as possible. The next day, because the cancer had advanced so much, doctors performed a hysterectomy.

This was the first operation I had had since an inexperienced resident multistitched me on the birthing table. Looking back, I should have been more cautious until I knew more about my condition, but I was too frightened to understand what to do, and the doctor seemed so anxious to get on with the process.

I walked through the door blind. I just wanted everything to be over and felt a certain exhaustion with life. I didn't care if my life ended right then and there. In the hospital, passing other rooms, I saw visitors gathered around loved ones' beds with green and blue balloons. Music streamed from one room, a song I used to love almost called me back into my body from this disappointing, frightening, hospital moment. But I was too burned out to offer myself solace. Abused by untrustworthy lovers, parental indifference, and physician hostility, I had had it! I had a beautiful little boy I felt I didn't deserve, so I said to myself, okay, tear out my inhospitable womb; I just don't care!

But as Buddha said, "Fortune changes like the swish of a horse's tail." I went from feeling imprisoned in the body to being released from it. I was paroled from hell into heaven. During the surgery, I found myself effortlessly floating above my body as I lay on the operating table. My surroundings were very clear, every detail was distinct. I could hear what was going on but could not speak. The energy that I call "Ondrea" saw this body and looked at it as if it were someone else's, at peace at a depth I had never before experienced. In a state of unwavering consciousness, the thought passed through me that this might possibly be a glimpse of death. It seemed I could get used to this pretty quickly. I was at one with the universe, nothing was absent, and no wish to be elsewhere arose.

I could see the doctors cutting me open. I felt nothing; I was more curious than concerned about what was going on down there with my body. The experience gave me a connection to something that went beyond my body. It was my first out-of-body experience. The realization that I was more than just a body gave me confidence in the dying process.

After my hysterectomy, I woke up in the maternity ward. If I had been grieving my inability to have another child, that would have really done me in. It was another medical fumble, quite insensitive and inappropriate for a person in post-op sterilization. To top it off, a nurse apparently thought I would like to wake up as Heidi, so she tied ribbons to the end of braids and applied to my lips bright red lipstick. When I was handed a small mirror in which to admire my transformation into a yodeling Swiss mountain girl, I was unsure why someone would do this to someone who had just had their reproductive organs removed.

I came to see my cancer as an initiation which directed my healing through the obstacles of the unkind mind, into the heart. My heart waited for me with open arms and a vastness of being that reminded me of the reason I took birth in the first place.

We are born into a life in which we own nothing, yet are directed to love nonetheless. It's easy to get lost in bifurcations along the path. We often need a co-pilot or someone to hold the ladder at least. I got both. Though we might be immersed in sorrow, unable to discern our face in the mirror, in great pain, that doesn't alter the fact that behind who we think we see in the mirror is the grace of our original face.

Grace may not always be pleasant, but it always brings us closer to our true nature. The prison of ownership is broken through when we recognize that some difficulties are actual blessings. Grace shows us we don't even own the breath. The breath, like the divine, owns us and when it departs, we go with it.

Ask Questions

It is usually presumed that a person faced with a serious diagnosis, before going further, would obtain a second opinion. Many may even seek a third opinion/treatment regimen that includes a naturalist, homoeopathist, experimental trials of less toxic treatments, and consultations with experts in natural chemotherapy and healing energy practices which balance the body and the mind.

If you are facing a serious diagnosis, please take a moment to ask your intuitive inner self, as if it were a crystal ball, what might be the next best step forward.

During workshops we were often asked questions about diagnosis and treatments:

Q: Whom, in the maelstrom of opinions and treatments, of prognosis and dosages, can I most rely on?

Nurses in general, and chemotherapy technicians, in particular, told me over the years to research all drug prescriptions because "doctors are overworked and don't always take enough time to read charts and check for contraindications in their medicines."

Q: I have heard so much about how a negative attitude can worsen illness. How do I keep my heart open, even when my heart sometimes closes?

And the heart replied, "The mind has a mind of its own. It judges us for being judgmental. It sometimes even judges us for not being judgmental. It's the human not-so-merry-go-round.

Deepen the root of mercy for ourselves. Watch the passing show that fear and resistance animates. If you remember nothing else, remember mercy. Illness is hard enough without long accustomed mercilessness muttering over our shoulder.

There can be a healing of the heart by not closing to ourselves, not judging or trying to find "an excuse" for being in so much pain. Letting go of what slams the heart is called "opening the heart in hell." It is part of the long pilgrimage, often initiated by some loss or illness, that takes us through grace, which brings us closer to our true nature. Part of that means to work, perhaps through meditation or prayer, certainly through acts of kindness and generosity, to stay balanced when the urge to escape closes our heart in anger at ourselves or the world in general.

We may be inwardly healed (get to the heart of the matter) well before the occurrence of a cure (a rebalancing of the body), if it is to be. On the other hand, I have known people who apparently got physically well but, because they so mercilessly continued to attack themselves and everyone around them, found themselves not whole. Love is often barely visible above the surface while a trembling fear of death may send out an unhealthy tension, a stubborn resistance which limits the beneficial penetration of medication, prayer, and even forgiveness.

People may lose their healing by not including love in their struggle for a cure. I have been told by one of the best alternative healers that perhaps because of the level of the aggression of their war against their illness, patients may send hatred into that which was calling out for a little kindness.

On a good day we get glimpses of a mercy that supports our wholeness even when we feel on the verge of shattering. I still remind myself to soften so as not to put myself out of my heart, to have mercy on this poor body and wobbly mind, to have love for myself, sending loving kindness into the pain and confusion, to be "whole, in pieces" as one teacher said.

When it comes to illness, there, of course, is fear but that is not all there is. There is a softening of the belly, a knowing in the body, in the very soul, that I am one of many thousands experiencing the same pain in the same body at this very moment. And I am, with all these others, sharing the One.

Q: What is the best thing I can do now after my diagnosis?

Mercy is the kindest form awareness takes. Explore with that mercy and awareness your dark path through the light. Make generous note of the map of consciousness, your attachment's insistence on its intentions and inclinations, the likes and dislikes which make us seasick by the end of the day. Liberation waits in the breath. How far into the body does the breath dare to go? How soft does the belly have to be to let life all the way in?

To uncover the uninjured in ourselves is to step out onto the ground of being, finding one's natural breath breathing itself in boundless space.

Q: How may one die with dignity and some control over the profoundly intimate process? For example, someone dying from AIDS who wished to exclude those who had been judgmental or hurtful during this person's breakthrough life.

One should designate an *ombudsman,* a spokesperson, a dedicated referee, to speak up when we may not be able to do so for ourselves. It is an extension of the Living Will. I have seen lovers guard each other at the deathbed so others cannot disturb their process. A strong guardian at the door can turn away even parents and mean-spirited family and "friends" who had been less than gracious, and more like rabid moralists, over the years.

On the other hand, it has repeatedly been observed that those who forgive the most profoundly seem to heal the deepest and quickest. Love is the "ombudsman" of the heart. Love can be the gatekeeper, struggling to keep the gate clear, while artfully opening wide the floodgates for the overflow of unfinished business just beneath the surface, the fetters and restraints which cause most of us to wake up frightened each day.

Q: Is learning of a diagnosis, or a prognosis, a good time to make life changes, or is it too late?

Don't wait for death to remind us to live. Death is a perfect mirror for life. It clarifies our priorities. It points the way to the heart from which the best sort of transformations naturally arise: compassion and loving kindness, generosity and courage.

Though many died in considerable peace with few loose ends (karmic debris) left over, it was noticeable that among those who had complaints, there seemed to be archetypal feelings of what some referred to as regrets about an "incomplete life."

Regrets

The first regret has to do with one's vocation.

A feeling of giving their life away to a job they did not like instead of doing some work they loved. They felt they should have gotten a job for the love of it and not only the money. A lawyer said he wished he had gotten into furniture design; his love was the smooth, even beat of his heart, at the whirring lathe. A much-rewarded autistic Broadway set designer wished he were an accountant, because numbers, as he said, "straighten my mind." For most, less dramatically, it could simply mean picking up a paint brush or taking a zafu (meditation cushion) out of the closet. I know of some who opened childcare centers or went back to school, as a student or a teacher. Or the luminous ones who disappear into the slums of India or Brazil with food and books for those in need and who we may hear about years later from a grown child or blessed wife after his death that, "His life was good. He helped a lot of people."

The second regret has to do with relationships.

Some wished they had gotten a divorce instead of staying with their partner for safety and financial reasons. Others might have gotten married. Some said they wished they had gotten different parents; others said they most regretted not being better parents themselves.

Many spoke of how distrust had left so many of life's gifts unopened. More than a few said they wished they had been less stubborn about creating a protective wall around themselves. Most of those who felt cheated by life said they'd been dealt off the bottom of the deck. They hadn't been given half a chance and were certain it was someone else's fault. They just couldn't find the door to the heart and had left themselves out in the cold.

The third regret was that they should have played more.

They should have made love more, served the needs of others more, been less afraid that love would steal their counterfeit selves, the person they had mentally constructed in order to be "someone of merit." When one is dying, pretense is the first thing to fall away as energy gathers in the heart and the fear that created the body begins to disengage.

Don't wait for tomorrow; being present leads to a life well lived.

SIX

As "My" Heart Becomes "The" Heart

SOMETIMES IN THE MIDDLE of the night there is only the idea of me and the breath in the dark room, "May all beings be free from suffering. May all beings be at peace. May all beings touch their suffering with mercy. May we all come be at peace. May all beings be free from suffering," and on the out-breath, "May all beings find their inborn peace. And have mercy on all the rest."

The pulse, from which all music comes, teaches the breath to pray in the darkness.

We are more lonely than alone in this prefrontal dawn, a first remembrance of what is to come. Someone very much like ourselves holds the breath like the baby Jesus, Rahula in swaddling clothes, Gopala in the second song before the earth is born.

Just the idea of me and the dark luminescence in the dream world of the first breaths after the dream of sleep.

May all beings be free from suffering, may all beings quietly between breaths follow the path across the horizon. The out-breath brings dreams to the mice sleeping in the walls. The breath that has no beginning and no end drifts through the song that precedes our birth and dispels the illusion that we are or are not who we think we are.

I do not sleep so well most nights. I am left alone with the moon slowly crossing from window to window. It is not a prayer as much as it is a holding of hands with all those others somewhere between being unable to sleep and simply being awake.

May all beings gather in the night to tell each other's secrets as their own. We don't know who is who, only that we were watching each other in our dreams and now in our waking we can barely hold back the love.

I used to be alone in the dark. Now the at-oneness gathers us together no longer wishing for dawn, no longer praising the formless. Now that we have each other calling into the shared heart, may each be free of their mercilessness with themselves; may all beings and nonbeings wish only the best for the next breath we share. There is a rumbling at the center of the earth as we breathe together breath for breath; there is a breath that stops before the next and lets us get off the dream as the next breaks over the horizon. In the dream another hovers just before the last is completed. Night exhales. All the songs wait to be born in the next breath. It is not only the living who see this coming. May all beings awoken or unable to break through find the mercy the breath and dreams might share. In the prayer that comes just before the dawn, there is no mind, the mind insists, only the sun and the breath waking us just before we die.

Just as I wish to be free of the pains that keep me waking each morning, and falling into sleep sometime later, may all those whose hands I can barely stand to let go of, whose love I cannot do without, remember that we are all and each in this next breath drawn. Loneliness is a furrow in the mind whose root disappears toward the center and gathers all our separate worlds into One.

May I be free of confusion and perpetual unkindness. Who is that I see in the mirror by the illusion of the morning's light? Who is that who, no matter how eloquent, cannot fully awaken and dreams their way through the day? All those others in the mirror are not waiting to become you, they are waiting to be released by your imaginings of yourself.

Something other than the next breath, the last tendrils of the dream, imagines something sacred. But nothing is sacred or otherwise. Intentions drip from the eaves of the last thought, kindness abounds . . . may that one I think does not love me, love themselves; may that one I cannot feel in my heart, feel their heart; may that one who hates me, not hate themselves; may that part of me that hates another part of me, have mercy; may mercy roll across the mind like a remembrance of some forgotten love; may all we have forgotten of vanishing light, of fleeting moments of love, gather to heal us . . . may all beings be free of mercilessness, may we reach out and embrace ourselves no matter how we resist it, hold us and whisper in our ear, "I love you. Please don't let my forgetfulness ever set us apart."

Listen to that voice in what passes for you say those words, "I love you." You know you have been waiting your whole life to hear those words in that familiar voice, waiting to be set free to love everyone else.

Night has delivered us to day. Don't let the illusion of separateness that darkness overcame cause you to forget.

Daytime has come; it is time for forgiveness.

SEVEN

Journey to the Top of My World

IN 1976 A COUPLE sent me a round-trip ticket to New Mexico because they felt sorry for me after my bout with cancer. So James and I headed off to the Wild West, Taos, New Mexico. It was a whole new world architecturally, linguistically, aesthetically, and stylistically. It had different food, a bigger sky, but as the old poets used to say, "It's still the same moon to remind us we are all born to find the same in all that appears different."

What I found were neighbors with big muscles and small dogs; turquoise ribbons woven through tribal pigtails of the peoples of the historic Native American Pueblo; the influence of the sacred Blue Mountain; and the hippy-cowboy-artist "Anglos" culture that I pretty much floated through at occasional free speech and anti-nuke rallies around the country.

The "locals" were unexpectedly welcoming. I appreciated, was even excited by, the adobe architecture, the *lattias, luminarias,* back-country dirt roads, and the beautiful early Spanish churches. The Northern New Mexican *comida* (cuisine) was a good experiment for my vegetarian diet. I was watched over by wide-open skies and remarkable starry nights. It was a whole new perceptual universe with the glittering Milky Way that stretched overhead. The Big Dipper tilted to pour the cosmos over the mountains and forests that whispered of the matrilineal inheritance of the sacred atmosphere. It was a good place for a new start.

My first volunteer job, north of Taos at the high mountain Native American Children's Home, was taking care of tribal children who had been removed from what the courts considered negligent households. One of the children I cared for was Geronimo's great-grandson; he was a sweet kid, like most of the "shelved" children.

I was particularly close to a nineteen-year-old boy who took me riding bareback as fast as we could go, up through the meadows and forests. I came to love these children and attempted to offer them, for a moment or two, in word and deed, some of the security they so much missed. There was a shared joy.

After the tribal home closed down due to lack of funds, I returned to my house-cleaning yoga. Because I had enjoyed working with patients back on the East Coast, I joined a local doctor's small death and dying group, and once again quite satisfactorily began visiting a few dying patients. I took the EMT course in night school to become an emergency medical technician and cleaned houses during the day. When I was in night school or had to babysit someone else's child to supplement my minimum wage, James was a latch-key child.

After thumbing rides for a year when my vehicle broke down, I saw an announcement for a cooking contest by which I might win a large freezer that I could sell to fix my non-running truck. The only problem was I couldn't cook. I had very few taste or olfactory receptors that worked well enough to tell when something was too spicy or bland, or which ingredient I might have left out, and there were only two recipes I could cook well from memory. Being from New England, I went for the fish I had made in years past, but to resonate with my new home, I included a few spoonfuls of mild salsa. I stuffed the fish with lobster and crab, kind spices, and a lot of loving "don't know," and submitted it to the Taos Chefs' Association.

I then, of course, completely forgot about the contest until one day while cleaning houses the thought came up, "Why not call and see who won the freezer?" It was a long shot, but I called the newspaper only to find out, after making them repeat my name twice, that I had miraculously been given the prize. All the chefs agreed my recipe was the best. I was astonished! My old army truck was happily up for a new transmission. But when they told me to come and pick up the freezer, I realized I didn't have the truck or the money yet to do so.

By chance I had met a lovely couple who ran a foster home for young children, and they were dearly in need of the freezer. Learning not to second-guess divine intervention, I gave the freezer worth $599 to them for $300, which was enough to fix my truck, and all were delighted.

I again began reading the Buddhist-oriented books I had started reading in my teens. Books on Zen Buddhism and the works of Gurdjieff and Ouspensky were the teachings that seemed to fit me best. Readings from Ananda Mayi Ma, Sarada Devi, and Ramakrishna opened the devotional door to my heart. Ram Dass's *Be Here Now* was a great delight. Ramana Maharshi's *Who Am I?* teachings cut through unclear thinking proffered by some contemporary teachers, and then came the boon of Nisargadatta's (loosely translated "Mr. Natural") *I Am That,* whose teachings on resting in being and letting go, "I Am," seemed to integrate many of the teachings which had led me to this moment.

These teachings fed me deeply, resonated profoundly within me, and echoed, some years later, the books Stephen gave me of Buddhist meditation teachers like Ajahn Chah and Jack Kornfield, Joseph Goldstein, and the loving metta master Sharon Salzberg.

With a newfound happiness, James made new friends and rode his dirt bike with his best buddy across the simmering Northern New Mexico mesas, through the vast, pinyon-studded, rolling desert, disappearing into hidden ravines. Our world was growing fuller.

I watched the rhythms of my breath come into balance with the rhythm of the enchanted land about me. Patience gradually became more like love, more than I ever would have imagined. I looked for guidance from the sacred unknown.

At Last

I joined the local death and dying group, led by a very heartfelt cardiologist. There were only six people that came to the meetings. With some ten years of experience, I was the old hand at working with patients; the rest were new to all this.

I was the only one comfortable visiting ailing people in their homes. The group looked up to me and asked a lot of questions about working with dying patients. Besides Elizabeth Kubler-Ross's groundbreaking books on death and dying, information on this subject was not readily available, and I was more than willing to hear more.

A general practitioner who joined the group wanted to support me in this endeavor and insisted I meet visiting expert Stephen Levine at a retreat coming up the next summer, at the Lama Foundation, twenty miles away. His Conscious Living/Conscious Dying workshops were highly regarded. I was still doing the house-cleaning yoga and had to save up for six months to afford this teaching. Oh, another "expert," I thought! But since I had never gone to any sort of workshop retreat, and because I trusted my doctor friend, I signed up even though I felt I probably knew more than this guy from out of town. I figured I could tell the workshop people things they didn't know.

I went to hear what this guy had to say. He was a kind fellow who taught a type of meditation I was unfamiliar with called "mindfulness" or "insight" meditation. I liked what was going on at the gathering of about sixty people and also liked the fellow's style; he was different and spoke in a Buddhist medium, a loving, empty kind of speech. He used a different sort of language than I was used to. And because I spoke and heard in what Stephen later lovingly referred to as "dyslexinese," I found it hard at times to catch all that he was saying. It was as if he came from another world. I took many more words to say what he could communicate more directly, succinctly. It was as if he could read my mind. He made me feel like my wise self. He told me I was a natural meditator and that I had insights it took many much longer to achieve. I thought he was saying these kind words just because he liked me. As it turned out, he more than liked me; he immediately loved me. And unbeknownst to me, I loved him too.

We later shared what only might be called a "psychic connection" that has been one of the hallmarks of our years together. At the end of the five-day retreat, as was the custom, the event was concluded with a Sufi circle dance where each person went hand-to-hand around the circle looking directly into another's eyes. You can imagine the love and energy that was generated. I had never looked so deeply into anyone's eyes before. The circle dance brought up a lot of emotions, seeing everyone's face melting into the one face—we are all the same, just with different stories.

When Stephen came to circle with me, I imagined this was probably the last time I would see him. But he did not pass me on to the next participant; instead he drew me away from the big circle, as we turned around and around our mutual axis. Stephen's heart was inside of me and mine was within him. I had never experienced this before. He said, "Let's get together down in Taos later." And so we did and have been together ever since.

At the small event, because of my story and cancer operations, I became "the house dying person," so to speak. I was surrounded by teary-eyed people who kept touching me! What world had I entered?! I know now it was just that love is attracted to a vacuum.

Because there was no touching in my family, being loved was one of my first, most difficult lessons. This teaching was amplified a year or so later, after the first time Stephen and I taught a large workshop together, when loving kindness descended like an angel on me, attracted to the love that I was discovering in myself.

After we spent a week together, Stephen had to fly back to California. He left me a photo of that rascal Maharaji, Neem Karoli Baba, his guru, and some wonderful music from the spirit-heart of Jai Uttal. At the time, I thought gurus were some kind of California invention, not to be trusted. But the music made me weep, and the dreams that were to follow blew what was left of my mind. In one dream Maharaji (in character, I was told later) wagged his grandfatherly finger at me, saying, "You're going to marry Stephen." He came to me in a dream the next night too, and I argued with him to no avail. I didn't know what was happening, but I felt loved and was on the "trip" of my life.

I got a postcard from Stephen, written on the plane on his way back home; he touched me with a love so similar to my dreams. I read the card a hundred times. I just could not believe that anyone could love me like that. I was surprised how much I believed him and how well he knew me—all in just a week.

Knowing how anxious I was about moving to a strange land where I knew no one and had no connections, Stephen said he would gather up his family and move to Taos. We spoke every day and night for a few weeks, as he was getting his life ready to move to New Mexico and set up living anew with my eleven-year-old son and me. His children, Tara, nine, and Noah, eight, were out of school for the summer and were given the option of moving back to California if they did not care for the new world of New Mexico. He said good-bye to his meditation group with a lovely closing ceremony, gave up his house, packed up his children and a few belongings, and headed out to our new home.

Meeting My Family

James and I waited for Stephen and his two children to arrive from California. I had been working for weeks on the house he and I had rented on his last visit. The phone rang, and there was a young girl's voice, "Ondrea, Dad, Noah, and I will be late because we got a late start from Santa Cruz." I was disappointed and nervous. I knew they were all okay, but I just had to be patient.

Within half an hour, the doorbell rang and when I opened the door, the three of them came streaming in laughing. I knew at that moment I had a new daughter, who was a natural actress. Noah came running in laughing and said, "Fooled you!" I knew I had another son who was a rascal on my hands. I was delighted.

I asked my new children to just call me Ondrea; I never intended to take the place of their biological mom. Since we had the children most of the time, I felt it important to maintain the "two-home principle." My job, as it seemed to me, was not to replace their previous family, but to expand it into this blended one.

I was fortunate and found myself rapidly falling in love with Stephen's children. I was interested in their fascinating hearts. Though, or perhaps because I considered myself less than a perfect parent, it seemed like a great opportunity to further learn and feed my heart with their beauty.

We, of course, had to learn to be friends first, and we did. As days turned into weeks and months, we blended and learned each other's ways. Stephen and I, most often, found a middle way to blend with the children's needs.

Coming from their open beach lifestyle, these California kids were more sophisticated than I was in some ways and less resistant than I would have guessed. Teenage Tara was the incarnation of girlishness and such a playful friend. She sang, acted, and was an all-around wealth of entertainment and information. We gossiped about boyfriends, modeled clothes, and sang popular songs. She even tried to teach me how to sing, but that turned out to be more fun and laughter than melodic.

She had an amazing ability to organize, which was always one of my weaknesses. She had a helpful knack for knowing just what present I should pick out for friends and those in my expanding family. She had a certain *panache,* verve, I lacked. She had style! Indeed, she had a quality of directness, like Stephen, that I admired. Fearless when it came to any issue, she would tell it like it was—talents which later were to serve her well in sales and managerial matters. A born communicator, she has become a powerful, single mother of four, and now CEO of her own company.

Tara also had a built-in compass that could find its way even in a new location, which was a trait I greatly admired as one used to getting lost even in a familiar surrounding, the labyrinth of dyslexia.

When she became pregnant, I was blessed to accompany her to many of her doctors' visits. With her in the car, we never had any trouble finding our way to her appointments or, with her directions, the subsequent three deliveries over the years.

Noah was younger, a skateboarding, wise-cracking Spiderman prankster whose ever-ready hugs and nudges greatly warmed me. He taught me how to play and not be so serious. Even today, he has a natural proclivity to find joy in whatever he is doing. He had a great laugh, which deepened mine as well, breaking one of the Ten Commandments of my childhood home: not to laugh. Teaching him to cook became a great bonding experience.

Noah also taught me how to be teased and aided in the cultivation of mercy and patience when he tripped over his boundaries or used them as a jump-rope. As a child, he fit into my own over-the-top energy quite well. As a natural communicator, he charmed everyone with his loving ways. He always knew how to get attention in a crowded room. When we first met, he took me crabbing, catching crustaceans in a rocky inlet, bonding ankle deep in the Pacific. When we went fossil hunting, he had endless interest in investigating further, being naturally inquisitive like his dad.

And now we watch him use the hardships of his early life (drugs and Juvenile Hall) as a path to wisdom and compassion to help others. He has become a fine writer, counselor, and teacher.

AN ASIDE

Though we speak of our children in this context, it is not our intention to invade their privacy or betray their confidences with a lot of vignettes from the familial merry-go-round. Though the temptation to regale the reader with heart-warming stories of the children or the blessings from our four grandchildren, Danielle, Gilbert, Mariah, and Peyton, we will relieve them of the need to explain themselves to their peers and just keep such stories in the archives of our hearts.

In the middle of the giddy circle of our new family was James's quick sense of humor, pulling the rug out from even the most serious situations. While we were watching the news together one night, James noticed a copy of one of Stephen's books on a bookshelf behind a war correspondent. "Yup," he said, "looks like they only read your books in war zones."

Gradually, rather than "Ondrea," I became "Mom 2," eventually morphing into "Mom too." Indeed in parts of Asia when a child has been deprived of a warm home and loving care by a parent who has become unavailable through illness, death, or addiction, the woman who comes along with open arms to help heal the wounds of that child is called a "karmic mother." Tara and Noah's biological mother, needing to go through some challenges of her own, was very supportive; she even referred to the kids as "our children." I never liked the "stepmom" label because it had acquired such a negative connotation. Originally, stepmothers were women who stepped up to the responsibilities of children whose biological moms were not around, but somewhere along the way the term got Walt Disneyized, twisted into the "Evil Stepmother" to her captive cinder-children. I was determined to mother this family of five as best I could.

I met Stephen in numbness and had much of myself to disinter. I was learning to relate *to* my emotions instead of just *from* them; to speak openly about certain painful thoughts without fear that Stephen might take away the keys to this new life—a life that was full and wonderful, as well as tough, at times, for both of us.

We learned how to use our "responders," as animals do, in a body language that encourages and discourages more harmful actions. When either of us laid our hand over our heart, for instance, the other knew immediately that pain, more than clarity, was being transmitted.

I think our communications may sometimes have been more difficult for him than me, and it's lucky he has a good sense of humor, because my dyslexia caused me on occasion to omit nouns and verbs from the sea of words floating in the air. I also tended to watch people's mouths, which caused me to lose a bundle of facial expressions and cues and to often misinterpret what was being communicated.

Observing my parents' body language, I used to watch their mouths to see if I was safe, and what might be their intentions, kind or otherwise. But with animals, I often found in their eyes a most immediate connection. Of course, some animals, as well as people, are more attracted to this directness than others. But it wasn't until I worked with patients that I tended to put my attention into their eyes, to show them they could trust me. Once I established that connection, there was no thought of self-protection.

Stephen and I always agreed, although not always at the same time. We never went to bed angry. Learning to be aware of the judging mind was a great aid in keeping the self-defensive tendency to blame at a minimum. Learning to be a human being is helped considerably when there are two at the game—a game where there is no net or table. Only a mirror and just the eyes of truth looking back into you. Confronted with your mind, there is nothing to do but surrender, which is what we did and, on a good day, find that what you are looking for is what is looking.

Standing at the edge of this world, I made breakfast for the crew, as Noah and James traded fours and growled for the morning repast. It was a lovely circle at a round table: bagels, omelets, and orange juice; trepidation and love; as something old and yet unhealed waited in this perfection for the other shoe to drop.

Before this I had only lived alone with my son, so I think we all hoped we would make it with this circus; we all had taken a giant step.

Stephen, Tara, and Noah had given up their established life to come all the way out to New Mexico to be with me. I wondered if they would hate me when the sheen wore off. Could my love break through their possible resentment? Their mother had no resistance or difficulty with them being out here, but I was no Dr. Spock. I was more like *Star Trek*'s Spock, a stranger in a strange land, following the Braille of love.

Be careful what you wish for because it might come with prepubescent children! It was a bit of a shock for James too, but Tara's vivaciousness and playful nature won him over, as did Noah's ticklish laughter. And though James at first may have wondered who these wild gypsy children were and who indeed was this other guy usurping his home, after about a year he and Stephen became particularly close. Both had the same lunatic sense of humor, and their relationship developed into exactly what James needed. Stephen was particularly concerned about James's chronic stomach pain and sat up with him on difficult nights when it periodically returned.

When Stephen adopted James, their nutty closeness drew my less-developed sense of playfulness along with them in the slip stream of their belly laughs. We all found something we cared for in each other. We were, as our dear friend Gerry Jampolsky, says, "doing our best to not make one illusion more important than another."

Stephen had given up his well-developed life in California, and I had given up my precious autonomy. This whole thing was bigger than the two of us, the five of us; the whole was bigger than the parts of us. It was a bit disorienting for me at times after years of a distinctly non-social lifestyle. And I wouldn't have done it for anyone but him, and clearly he would not have done it for anyone but me. We dove in together. I taught him to untuck his shirt, and he taught me to untuck my feelings. It was as though we gave each other swimming lessons.

EIGHT

A Wild and Simple Coincidence

THE AWARENESS CULTIVATED THROUGH devoted service clears the throat to sing the song we were born to sing. To learn how not to turn away from the suffering of other sentient beings is to, as they say, "open the heart in hell." This service to others, this gradual awakening, increases our capacity to care for others and also to share this openness in personal relationships.

What a wild coincidence that when Stephen and I met, besides his well-established Buddhist meditation practice, he was also exploring a similar devotion to the path of service. Now I am not saying I prayed for Stephen, but he did say he was praying for me.

Stephen didn't often refer to God or Jesus, though each, he said, had offered him valuable teachings—stepping-stones across the river of forgetfulness—that brought him to his present worldview. He said many use the term "the Beloved" for lack of any term big enough to personify the yearning for the direct experience of the luminescence of our deathless nature.

Sometimes, in this remarkable though difficult incarnation, still given to bouts of impermanence, one may find an extraordinary connection to the well-being of one's beloved, the Beloved. When being loving becomes even more important than being loved, true devotion is experienced.

The first time I heard him say "the Beloved," it took my devotional heart to a level deeper. It was perfect.

"The Beloved" is a term that faces in all directions. It serves particularly well in the mystical, devotional aspect, which seeks the "hidden mysteries." When one turns toward these perennial mysteries, a common root reveals a Oneness: the Beloved. It is used to describe the divine in many faiths from Christianity to Islam and as an adjective to denote reverence from the Buddha to the Great Spirit of innumerable Native American tribal peoples. It reminds us of something so much greater than we imagine ourselves.

When we refer to our true nature, out of wild exasperation for something to contain its immensity, we find the term "the Beloved" fits perfectly into the heart and shares the breath of unconditional love. It is a term beyond definition, but not beyond experiencing. It is not anything you think but that through which thought flashes on its way beyond thought. It is the inconceivable enormity of our own beingness.

Without gender, the Beloved has no specific form. It is not different from anything. How could it be him or her when it is the unified suchness out of which differences arise? It is *Itself* itself.

Sometimes when we chanted *Ram Shri Ram Shri Jai Jai Ram* from one ventricle or *Gate Gate Paragate Parasamgate Bodhi Svaha* from the other (The Heart Sutra, gone, gone, gone beyond, gone altogether beyond, to the other shore . . . Enlightenment Hail!) for an evening, my body would become so light I thought I might float away.

At first I thought my devotional practices might conflict with Buddhist insight meditation. But I was learning to be mindful of the breath from which words and actions often unconsciously arise. The more I explored their differences, the more I experienced their similarities appearing mutually supportive.

For me, both arrived at the same place, meeting where pure awareness was indistinguishable from pure love, where the quiet mind floated in unconditional love, where the Dalai Lama, considered by many to be a living Buddha, has often said, "My only religion is kindness."

I was learning that what was at the center of the heart was not just God or the Beloved but the Nameless truth of our essential nature, our radiant suchness.

My prayers were changing. They were for the healing of the shared heart. Sending prayers out that all sentient beings might become more compassionate. For years I chanted:

> *"The power of God,*
> *Love is within me;*
> *The grace of God,*
> *Love surrounds me."*

What the Buddha had to confront and overcome on his way into indescribable Grace was the separation between the viewer and the viewed, entering the indefatigable suchness from which compassion flows so easily; the Original Mind before the separate mind comes into view. He had to relinquish not only our obvious addictions to pleasure and self-satisfaction, but also our negative attachment to suffering; our resistance and general dissatisfaction; nagging unworthiness; and the difficult-to-release, over-indulged identification with fear, greed and dishonesty, without which we might find ourselves difficult to recognize.

In perhaps the greatest of all devotional poetry, in the spectacular longings of Rumi, Kabir, Mirabai, and Rabia, the Beloved is all that is sought. But to all who seek their own true nature, their own enormity, whether Hindu or Buddhist, Christian or Jew, Jain or tribal peoples everywhere, even the atheist or agnostic, what is sought is the irreducible vastness of our deepest truth.

And in hands cupped like the frontal lobes in prayer, we find the capacity to transform our pool of tears into the Ocean of Compassion. We look into the eyes of what so many call the Beloved and discover what the Buddhist call their Original Face.

Beneath the Sargasso Sea of afflictive thoughts and emotions tangled on the surface of the mind, beneath the ordinary grief of our self-image, beneath our hunger and disappointment, lies the miraculous *isness,* the ever-comfortable ground of Being, the self-effulgent Presence within presence.

To know the Beloved, we need to let go of all that is unloved, judged, forged from old mind clingings. The Beloved is the unconditional love beyond the conditioned mind. Unconditional love is a natural manifestation of being. When there is nothing to obstruct love, love simply is. It is our homesickness for the truth, which draws us towards the Beloved.

Some ancient thrill is called forth in surrendering our secret wretchedness and obvious suffering. Hindrance after hindrance yields the right of way to our true heart. Unobstructed grace roams the labyrinth singing of the Beloved.

I don't know why I am so drawn to the Beloved. It doesn't make any sense. It's all out of proportion. Sometimes I call it Jesus, Mary, Krishna, Kuan Yin, or God, though it seems always personified in those who act with spiritual courage, motivated by mercy, compassion, generosity, gratitude, and love.

It is so hard to let go of the ecstasy of self-discovery. We only last a moment: aspirants and Mayflies humming the Beloved, face down in the luminescence. Not fit for anything but love, homesick for the Beloved.

Never easy in my mind, I longed for my true heart, to know the Beloved, to become my true heart.

Stephen told me that before he met the Buddha he sought his true heart in the remarkable tale of the Bhagavad Gita. Each morning he compared a stanza, one gatha at a time, in three somewhat different translations, and drank deeply from the divine cup of Krishna's epic poem, breathing in and out of the heart center.

After work he chanted just beneath his breath, *Om Tat Sat,* which may be translated as "everything is Everything," the center of the Universe everywhere we looked, directing me home. It said, "I am That."

It was a reminder that having become so small and proud of it, it is easy to forget how infinite the spirit.

When forgetting our enormity, we say, "I am only this!" But it does not take long before impermanence reveals the world-weariness of any idea of "I," or any idea of "this" which does not almost immediately slip into becoming something else.

The Buddha's First Noble Truth pointed out that sometimes trying to be anything at all, without it changing in a millisecond, is downright depressing. The innate gift the Sufis called "the open secret" was not a secret at all, but the great neglected truth that we are "That."

Reflecting for some time on "I am That," Stephen was unable to contain all that was unfolding, and was barely able to keep his head above the undertow of impermanence until soon only the *amness* remained, only the presence by which all else is known.

Following the course of evolution, our chant begins in the belly and rises through the heart, manifesting behind the brow in sudden wordless understandings. Unable to find a word which can contain the totality in the poverty of language, the boundless whole is called That.

Though we may sing from the joy of discovery, what we are singing about is not one's own, but the commonality of the spirit. The song we took birth to sing.

We are That and that is what we sing about.

A New Union

And as we sang we set up a new household. We all had to adjust our frame of reference in order to maintain our steadiness on the balancing beam. I had been a single parent all of my child's life, and Stephen, since his divorce, had also been a single parent for more than half of his children's lives.

Nothing as world-changing as the merging of families comes about without its ups and downs, hopes and disappointments, resistance and victories. In time, as we all became accustomed to each other's weird beauty, there were wonderful moments that bonded the whole in a comfort that soothed the savage beast in us all and germinated into a lovely unity.

In order to establish a strong bond, without getting ensnared in expectation—the kind that feeds our disappointment and suggests depression—we sometimes allowed a misshapen circle to form, without the push and pull that removes the sad flesh from the decomposing bone, causing—as we have seen so often—people who once loved so well to hate so intensely.

To discover the catalyst for a blended family, a lot of learning and unlearning, giving and surrender is required, an intention to treat our beloveds as the Beloved. Of course, this is easier said than done, but on a good day there was an aspiration to share what lies beyond our long-cultivated self-protectiveness, to be so generously surrendered, as to give ourselves away to each other as one might the divine, for which we got the "Good try, but no gold medal" award.

The Dalai Lama once laughingly said that to be in a relationship is to give up half your freedom. And we would add, what real freedom do we have until we surrender what holds us back—to realize the half-life of our indestructible luminescence, our deathless enormity?

It was a radical change for me to go from a small old adobe house without plumbing and a windy outhouse, chopping my own firewood, carried in my broken-down old army truck, having to check myself in and out of the hospital for my cancer operation the year before, to a "real" house on a "real" street. I was working two jobs, attending to dying patients as time allowed, and moving in tandem with my beloved to a larger house in picturesque Santa Fe. With three children to meet, merge, and care for, this new life offered a daily regimen of love and bewilderment, which both frightened and entranced me.

Our desks snuggled up against each other as we worked together on the book *Who Dies?* Along with new family permutations, there were the two phones, dozens of patients, providers that wanted us to give talks, workshops and retreats, enough money for a change. There was a large spiritual family of Stephen's old friends, many of whom were prominent writers and teachers, and I was discovering daily what it was that Buddhism actually meant, and how to find its root in myself. Not to mention becoming the instant co-chair of the Hanuman Foundation Dying Project, publishing a newsletter every few months. I was a stranger in a strange land, but it was just right.

I dressed and spoke differently and had a different energy than most of Stephen's tribe, but that didn't seem to bother him at all. In fact, what he called my "natural wisdom" seemed to offer him a much-appreciated balance.

When he first asked me to teach with him, I was scared, honored, and fascinated. He knew when I heard some of the hard stories of people in dire distress that my heart would embrace them and that an encouragement to forgive themselves would naturally pour from me. He knew me better than I did, and he was right. When we returned home from the first retreat, I had a new occupation. He said I was one of the best natural therapists he had ever seen.

I was learning how to identify states of mind, to note their rising and falling, and at the same time, was perhaps, for the first time looking my emotions straight in the eye.

Of course, melodramas arose from blending the families and the difficulties of finding a mutually agreeable center to counterbalance, with kindness and understanding, the children's natural urge to return to the comfortable known and their old convenient lifestyle. For James, it was the one-on-one of just him and me, and for the California wildings, it was their beach town, old friends, and predictable life.

Sometimes it was a flock of angels, at other times a school of sharks, making decisions like what programs to watch, which friends to play with, whose parent will "have the last word," which bedroom is nicer—all the attractions and repulsions of magnets turning from end to end.

When it came to the near-perfect hallucination of lectures and workshops, students, health professionals, meditators, dying patients, and grieving caregivers, I was learning how to listen without my mind getting in the way. To hear, without my old insecurities blocking my heart's reception of their issues and needs, love.

I stopped distrusting myself so much and got down to what the Buddha called "the work to be done." I came to know that doubt and fear were "mind only," and I continued on the path that was leading so many toward a better life and a greater sense of liberation.

Stephen had taken me into a whole new world of feelings and self-expression, living teachings I had only read about. I started learning how to be with groups, by sitting next to him and silently sending love and encouraging self-forgiveness into the room. It was an important part of my practice of becoming fully human. I was slightly psychic, and sometimes with my eyes closed I would direct my attention to individuals I felt could use some support. It really surprised me when, after workshops, those people often came up to me and asked me if I was transmitting some sort of love to them. They even thanked me, at times, for clearing their heart so they could express for the group their grief process and how the meditations worked for them.

Stephen was one of the first people who saw who I really was. He knocked me out! He had superb confidence in what he called "my developing shamanic abilities." He was a gift from the Universe that I could hardly believe could love me so.

A Gathering of the Tribe

After Stephen and I had been together a few months, there was going to be, in a place not far from where we lived in Taos, the first

Bandara—a celebration of the presence and death of the group's Maha Guru (Master Teacher and divine ally Maharaji, Neem Karoli Baba)—at which I was going to meet Ram Dass, one of Stephen's oldest and closest friends with whom he often taught. I had heard many stories about how tough Ram Dass could be with people he was trying to feel out. He would test your weak spots and check out the blockages to your heart. I had also heard he was one of the wisest, most loving beings in the world. But he was a *guru*! And that word rubbed me the wrong way. I was judgmental of the judgment of gurus and any control games they might be playing.

But Ram Dass was very kind and accepting of our relationship. Even so, because I had thrown myself into the fire of this group's teaching, as a service he was tough on me as a teacher, and showed me ways of getting closer to the truth and being able, when working with an audience, to do the same for them. I learned another level of being, and on occasion, even felt the grace of his teacher Maharaji—a grace that has at times guided me through the years. This first inundation in a devotional yoga taught me wonderfully useful teachings in surrender. I had always been so defensive that surrender seemed to me to be defeat. I came to learn it meant letting go, releasing negative attachments and the addictions to our suffering.

Because Ram Dass was one of Stephen's closest friends, it was important to me to be accepted by him. It took awhile for R.D. (as he was referred to by his friends) to understand my dyslexic ways, but because we both loved Stephen, it was a devotional triangle, and we got used to each other's differences. Once in a while, just to get things moving, I would say back to him what I heard in his mind. He would shake his head like a horse shooing away a deerfly, or a parent to its child, and say lovingly, "Now don't do that!" We came to appreciate each other like friends in a sandbox. R.D. complimented me on our teaching together and said Stephen and I had something unique that he hadn't seen in other couples.

I was honored and told him what a blessing the teachings he had passed on to me were, and what a help they proved to be for groups hungry for the spirit who were turning toward opportunities for service. I found that the differences and similarities between Buddhist and Hindu worldviews stretched my mind and bared my heart; they made me grow into a whole human being. I learned to love more and deeper without need of some loved object but just to love for no reason at all. And the tribe expanded exponentially with the increased energy in the heart center.

Relationship Yoga

One of the games, experiments in consciousness, we used to engage in was when our eyes unintentionally met in passing, Stephen and I would stop what we were doing and enter into each other's eyes. We would just let go into love and allow any blockage to surrender or drop away. This exercise is not recommended when one is driving or cooking a three-minute egg, but otherwise it can become a bonding practice that cultivates qualities like patience, concentration, and open-handedness.

We had an abiding conviction in each other. So after three years of providing meditation and Conscious Living/Conscious Dying workshops and retreats, with our early San Francisco coordinator, Allen Klein, beseeching us, we offered our first relationship weekend. (Allen now offers humor-based workshops on lightening the load of illness.) Then, the angel, Susan Barber, one of the most hospitable naturally thoughtful, generous beings I have ever met, adroitly took over the practical matters and skillfully organized the workshops nationwide. My compadre, kind Arthur Martin, with whom I shared so many stages of healing, brought inherent logic and a supportive nature. He was a great inspiration.

A few old friends, along with a surprisingly full house, attended the first of these weekends. Their nods and smiles were a considerable encouragement. Also attending was our dear friend Ram Dass, who would be a central player (once as the minister and the next as the best man) in two of our three wedding ceremonies.

After the workshop ended late Sunday afternoon, R.D. was sparkling and actually a bit surprised we could pull it off so well on our first try. He took us to his secret Chinatown egg roll connection. He had just gotten his old Plymouth Valiant out of the shop, and with the Bee Gees blaring from the car speakers, we flew over the San Francisco hills. A moment to remember! Even now, whenever we hear the Bee Gees, it causes a Pavlovian response of love for him.

We were all ecstatic and it felt like we were in the youthful exuberance of a college outing. But then again, very little we did with Ram Dass was ever particularly typical. It was more extra-normal, than ordinary. He is an amazing person who loves the word, and is the word, "delicious."

One afternoon at a relationship workshop, Stephen shared with a room full of couples a new and reassuring teaching that could achieve the power of celibacy, what in India is called "brahmacharya," by complete commitment to only one's mate. With this practice there is no fantasizing of another person, just a looking away, a diverting of one's eyes from any object of sexual desire. Stephen pointed out that this aspect of devotion can be as strong as the dedication one might have for the Beloved, or that evinced by the commitment to one's teachers or one's lifelong spiritual practice. "It is the type of commitment which can turn a relationship into a 'mystical union,'" he said. A commitment in which we first relate to our partner as our beloved and then gradually approach them as the Beloved, beginning to see them as aspects of God, or the vastness, or whatever the heart can translate into the essence of love. Using relationship as a yoga to take one beyond the mundane, to the truth that nurtures insight, to the wordless understanding that propels evolution.

Seeing your partner as the mirror of your heart, in whatever stage it might be, you share your potential to go beyond the mind, into the heart of the matter.

I think very few in the group had ever heard of this relationship concept. The group's energy was beginning to buzz. You could see in many couples' eyes the possibility of transforming suffering to grace.

An Expanding of the Tribe

Before a relationship retreat for six hundred couples at the Omega Institute, we heard that Baba Olatunji was just finishing up a workshop there. Because he was a strong pulse in my prepubescent coming out, I thought it would be a touch of grace to meet him—and grace it was. I thought I was going to meet a world-famous African drummer, whom I had danced to and whose records I treasured as a teenager, but I encountered a good deal more than that. As soon as I saw him at the head of a classroom, which was emptying at the end of a session, I was overwhelmed with the same feelings I experienced previously when coming into the presence of a spiritual master. His eyes were filled with such love. His hand extended to us was indescribable softness. His voice made us drop to our knees before him. He put his hand on our heads and blessed us. He was what spiritual voyagers call "the real thing."

In the back of the room, his old students lingered, waiting to see if we could truly see him. They were laughing and nodding at our wish to offer such a being a full prostration, to demonstrate our recognition of his realized state. If we had not been obligated to begin our retreat in an hour, we might have spent more time with him and may have even followed him to his next teaching, which we sensed would have as much to do with the beat of our hearts as the multi-leveled soul he brought out of a drum.

Just to tickle me with the size of my true family, from this mystery arose the sweet irony that during my wild teenage dancing in the '60s (while Stephen was an editor of the *San Francisco Oracle*), along with Olatunji, I most liked to dance to the band, Quicksilver Messenger Service, who it turns out was managed by one of Stephen's oldest best friends, Ron Polte. His office also managed Big Brother and the Holding Company, which included Janice Joplin, my old emotional release valve.

Ron was a remarkable friend of Stephen's who once, for instance, "just to blow his mind," bought him, back in the day, a classic old Ford pickup truck and left it in his driveway, with a big heart painted on it. Stephen told me Ron had taught him a great deal about kindness and generosity. They are still the very best of friends. Today Ron shares his home-baked scones with us, which Stephen wryly comments are a lot healthier than some of the other stuff they used to share.

Of Course, We Got Married

Stephen asked me to marry him two weeks after we met. I wanted to marry him, but I always said I would never marry again. And what did that silly piece of paper mean anyway? I was wrong again! The formal commitment was a vow and in his world that really meant something. It did to me too. He was the heart of my life.

We waited a year, testing the ground, exploring our terrain, and then the following May, one year after we met, he wrote our marriage vows:

"I offer you my fear, ignorance and old clinging in emptiness and love.

"I offer you my mind's ever-changing tides to grow together,
uncovering the living truth in each moment we can open to.

"I offer you my heart's love and commitment to help guide us to the other shore.

"My life comes full circle with this vow, to work this lifetime together to go to the
Beloved, to come to the love that goes beyond form."

In the big dome at the Lama Foundation, where we had met, we were married by Ram Dass, surrounded by dozens of our friends and our three bewildered children. Just to show off, during the ceremony, after a long drought on the Sangre de Cristo Mountains, the great thunderheads released their bounty. The drought was over. We were married again a week later by a Hispanic female judge and twice more over the years, including once, with all the participants included, by a Methodist minister at a relationship retreat.

After the ceremony we stayed at a friend's casita in Santa Fe for the weekend. Apparently, the ceremony was not quite over. We set up a few pictures on the dresser beneath the mirror. We thanked dear Maharaji for his capacity as a matchmaker, and just as we were about to go to bed, we noticed a moth had alighted on his picture. We noted how the moth and Maharaji were both "phototropic"—each drawn irresistibly to the light.

Some hours later we were awakened by the sound of what seemed like an enormous bird, perhaps an eagle, beating its wings against the terrazzo floor. As the wings thundered against the ceramic floor in the darkness, we reached out to touch each other as a reality check, and we heard in the roar of the wings Maharaji's message to us, "Only fear can destroy this relationship." We listened silently for some minutes before returning to sleep. In the morning we compared notes and found we both received word-for-word the same message and had precisely the same experience. In the morning light the moth was dead on our teacher's photo. The moth of the moment had told us all we needed to know. Hundreds of times since that experience we have recalled that warning to help clear the mind and open the heart anew.

This was the first lesson in the alchemy of relationship. To transform the frightened, separate, and numbed into the confident and unified. To convert the ordinary into the extraordinary, transforming our ordinary grief and separation into an inseparability of hearts. I was thirty-three years old and finally had found my real family. I had discovered my tribe.

NINE

Peaceable Kingdom

IMAGINE YOURSELF LOST IN the forest, when you sit down and just surrender, give your body and mind back to creation, the Uninjured essence of things envelop you, leaving nothing absent. This may also happen in meditation, in prayer, in hours and days of chanting a sacred name, or when a well-developed athlete "hits the wall" and goes through it.

The Uninjured is like a well-worn path we barely remember until the Eye of Beauty opens, and we see the beauty that has been there all along. It is our *Logos*, the wisdom factor, our forgotten way home, the divining principle by which we see into what sometimes appears to be a lost universe.

It is the balance in the heart between life and death. It is the original uninjured and uninjurable background and sub-center of all we perceive. The injured/the torn away/the attached floats face up in the ever uninjured and uninjurable luminescence by which we see. It is here, in the clear duality that separates light from shadow, that we find what we have been looking for. So many lost moments settling back into "the process-with-our-face-on–it" as we discover the life we have been searching for within us.

The Uninjured in myself, as it is for many mind-scramblers and dyslexics, seems to be the natural world, the animals and plants, mountains and rivers of my forest nature, and my tears for the creatures of the leaf litter who have on occasion died in my lap during my walkabouts.

The Uninjured is the spaciousness of being, the natural luminosity in which our thoughts and feelings float; the direct experience of which allows us a glimpse of our true nature. Best yet, it is the time between the moments between breaths when I am not waiting.

I had always wanted too many animals because since I was very young their presence comforted me. I could communicate with animals without all those pesky words breaking our connection like it did with people. But I had never lived in a large enough space to accommodate this fantasy. Stephen was supportive; in fact, when he was in school he considered being a zoologist. His early books about tending a wildlife sanctuary for The Nature Conservancy and later editing another about mending injured wildings were evidence of his commitment to wildlife causes.

I had cats and dogs but never the Peaceable Kingdom of my dreams. I can barely keep from laughing as we write this, but it began surreptitiously with a gift for Stephen. Father's Day was coming and I wanted to get him something lovely and quite unexpected that I knew he would adore. So before he got home from one of his talks, I searched about and found a miniature donkey, which would grow to be 28 inches tall at the shoulder.

The donkey was able to stand up in the back of our SUV and he brayed all the way home. People in the cars passing by, on the three-hour trip, kept beeping their horns and waving and laughing at this remarkable sight. Surprise!

He was a sweet addition to the family and consoled me many times when I was so saddened by the grief shared by dying patients. Sometimes I would go out into the field, and he would come over to me, placing his head on my shoulder as I would hug him and cry. He never walked away. I could sit with him as long as I needed.

Once looking up from the succor of Dharma Donkey's presence, across the pasture I saw Stephen nursing old Donkey-Ma, dying in his arms. Donkey Ma and I often slowly rode the fence, watching birds and beasts finding their niche, away from the eyes of man and long-eared friends alike. Her sorrel filly frolicking about would pass us, scooting around in circles and back again, kicking up the dust beside us, as I sat astride her broad back.

She may not have had quite the nobility of a horse, but she was a sainted donkey who would even breastfeed others' offspring.

Interestingly, when Stephen met my parents for the first time, when they came to visit us in what we called the "Taos animal farm," I thought all the sweet beasts might make their visit better than they expected. In fact, when they came through the door, after passing by a couple of inquisitive llamas humming to them over the fence, my mother gave me a unexpected hug. It was the first time she had ever hugged me. It was uncomfortable and gratifying. But they still couldn't look me in the eye.

Over the next few years a menagerie of miniature donkeys, llamas, a sizable bird aviary, a particularly delightful mule, a miniature horse, chickens, ducks, and geese followed the trail of my desire to our home.

Native Freedom

To own a living creature is akin to imagining one can own the land, a piece of the living planet, but the county clerk is not a holy herald, cannot convey the earth's corpuscles or describe the mineral gene-alogy of a grazing pronghorn. The native peoples knew they could not own the land because they could not control it. Man in the present twenty-first century delusion imagines that he can possess the land, so he and the land erode in direct proportion to each other's lack of native freedom. A donkey/mule/chicken, like a piece of land, responds in direct proportion to the respect and kindness it is offered. Each willingly offers its energies in response to love.

On one occasion, I heard shots fired about a half mile away. But by the time I got there, a deer lay dying as the poachers ran off. I sat with that dying white tail deer as she bled out, as the world bled out, as the heart we all share emptied like a goblet. A silence enveloped us as I tried to match my breathing with hers, in-breath hard and pained, then slowing, out-breath stuttering and stopping, coughing some blood; then she released her spirit out into the unbroken blue sky.

All our gut shot wilderness left bleeding its last breaths into a rusty sky. As part of all that dies, that is abused, that is met with cold indifference because of our unwillingness to turn inward to find how suicidal we are; to stop killing ourselves one piece at a time, as manatee, fox, coyote, salmon, and the stag elk that roams our pinyon forests. And as the porpoise and the sea otters I coaxed off the rocks and onto the Pacific beach. And the lion who came to wish me well on my sixtieth birthday who then disappeared over the mountain behind the house and became a cloud in the azure field of the sky.

Amongst the animal family, as another teaching in warmth and patience, we had a timber wolf whose eyes I was instructed not to look into, or he might take it as an act of aggression, even a challenge. But of course we found that once she felt our care for her, she opened her gaze to us. Even though a subliminal fear may have passed between us, she seemed comforted each time we came into contact; she would scan our eyes to check out our state of mind and let us know we were safe, that we were family.

During these wonderful days that I was being taught by donkeys and Buddha, my farm work expanded even as I continued to help arrange retreats and workshops, and maintained long-established communications with dying patients and those in deep grief.

Tandem Teachings

Besides working side-by-side for more than thirty seven writing books about healing and the growth of a merciful awareness, like *Who Dies?*, *Healing into Life and Death*, *Guided Meditations*, *Meetings at the Edge* (recorded conversations from our twenty-four-hour Dying Project grief phone), and the meditative relationship guide *Embracing the Beloved*, Stephen and I also presented a number of workshops and retreats each year.

After the first few years, the weekend Conscious Living/Conscious Dying workshops, offered in many large cities, grew to about five hundred to seven hundred participants for two eight-hour days. These workshops opened many doors for some and closed the last door for many more. The retreats were five-day intensives—often a thirteen-hour pressure cooker—for hundreds of people, held at retreat centers in natural settings. As the groups grew and many participants returned for our yearly offerings in New York City, San Francisco, Seattle, and Washington, D.C., local groups of volunteers (some of which evolved into hospices) organically formed to serve the dying and grieving in each city. As much as one-third of any group was on scholarship because of the terrible financial and emotional expense. This encouragement to service was an idea Stephen inherited from years of teaching with Elizabeth Kubler-Ross before we met. It just felt right.

Workshops and retreats were always a learning opportunity and quite tiring for us afterward, not only because of the teaching work and the absorption of many people's grief, but from the fatigue of the long hours of organizing. Indeed, this was in the early years, before we had a regular, local staff at each venue finding the best locations, getting people signed up, getting the happiest vegetarian cooks, buying food, etc.

At times, when the going got tough in "the big room," we also had to lend emotional support to the volunteers and staff. It was a lot to expect of these young yogis and middle-aged psychotherapists, upon hearing some very sad stories, not to be assaulted by their own unfinished business. Even the cooks sometimes got noticeably stressed from overhearing the emotional upwelling from the main hall. The cooks always knew when it was "heating up" in the gathering because the amount of food consumed increased exponentially. Huge amounts of food were often required for people to handle the very personal unburdenings about the deaths of children, suicides, the grief of sexual abuse, the witnessing of loved ones dying in fires, the diminishment of aging parents, and the uncovering of feelings of loss—our original grief, long hidden in the marrow.

Part of my other mindedness was that I was "a finder." People who had lost things of importance often came to me to retrieve them. This is, it seems to me, because I have been given a particular attention to details, an ability to deconstruct the whole into its parts, to see the individual pieces of the jigsaw puzzle without being distracted by the intended picture.

Once, at a long retreat at the Breitenbush Retreat Center in the Oregon woods, a lady came back from a walk bereft, crying that she had somehow lost her diamond wedding ring out in the forest. She had spent hours searching for the treasured object around the log she had been sitting on to no avail. Though she felt it would be impossible, having heard of my quirk for "finding things," she asked me to help. We went back to where she had been sitting in the woods, and as she scanned the area, certain it was gone, within a short time I found it!

At times when we first did workshops, people would approach me to tell me I came to them in dreams. One person said they had a dream the night before of a Native American woman who told him he was loved and okay as is. When he came into the meeting room, I was greeting people at the registration table wearing tribal braids with a meditation blanket wrapped around me for warmth, which he said was just the way he had seen me in his dreams. I told him I never have any such intentions, that perhaps he had seen a photo of me somewhere. But because he was so disturbed, he left.

In each workshop or retreat there were always groups of individuals who were working with similar issues. Each group seemed to have a predominant aspect of grief that called for exploration: dying parents, dying children, sexual abuse, the profound commitment of AIDS couples (who having fought their way through prejudice and the long travail of midnight emergency room visits—all that taking turns dying!) finally having to part. One after another, the profound losses of loved ones abandoned to suicide or stolen by murder, the astonishing commonality of sexual abuse, the common grief of divorce and betrayal. Tending too to those who tend to others, the caretakers and volunteers who needed to share their stories.

In each gathering there was the spiritual hunger to know themselves, to find a spiritual practice that worked for each to open up to the hesitant acceptance of our shared mortality as we look at our life and exclaim, "How can I not be among you?"

Each person wondered how to stay afloat and not drown in the "Reservoir of Grief." No one is exempt from the oneness of pain and love. Days devoted to how best to serve what Buddha said were the inevitabilities of life, illness, old age, and death.

To increase the tools available to work through these issues, as there was so much deep feeling in the longer retreats, the group often meditated up to three or four hours a day. Many were guided meditations directing awareness and mercy into specific areas and issues, including many Buddhist mindfulness meditations which, for some, began lifelong "sitting practices."

We chose to not provide meat at the meals as it tends, like sugar, to make people sluggish and keep people from playing their edge. Indeed, it has been employed by some meditation masters to bring down students whose energy (*kundalini*) may have overwhelmed them.

Just to raise the stakes, people were asked to stay in silence except to share in the main hall, so as to amplify the internal static and buried sorrow. Of course, some drank a lot of coffee and tea, as is the mediator's way to support long hours of practice; a few sat with their ghosts in the empty hall well into the night. The monks and nuns who occasionally attended these retreats drank their share of caffeine as well. But most, exhausted by the considerable emotional outpouring of the day, could be heard snoring, without difficulty, as one walked down the nighttime hallways.

There were always some people in the group who were dying, accompanied by their participating loved ones. There were psychotherapists, nurses, hospice volunteers, and the family members who were attending the dying. There were also grief counselors and those who simply came to overcome their fear of death. Blessedly, those who had been coming to these events for years were able to turn to those most broken by their loss and hold them in their hearts. They listened with the mercy and skill of quiet compassion, not advising as much as allowing the healing to occur in a safe place.

Also in attendance were a few heartfelt therapists we could count on to attend to those having a particularly difficult time. Those who like Kuan Yin, the Merciful One, can "hear the cries of the world," were able to sit casually nearby one who was venting their awful sorrow, available to hold someone in pain and stay open to horrible, sometimes unlistenable stories of abuse and not lose their ground.

Naturally we were quite disturbed at times, particularly when stories of sexual abuse gradually became part of the daily grief work we attended to. The first time the abuse was brought up, Stephen wept for more than an hour. I sat beside him weeping on and off, a ten-ton weight on my chest. We could barely move; we were so glad we could be there for them, so shocked at the inhumanity. Luckily, we had each other for consolation.

Sometimes, when the program ended, there was a line of participants who had waited to ask a particular question. Drained by the days of almost preternatural energy, we were often too tired to think, many of our replies arising from a partially exposed intuition. It sounds more heroic than it actually was because the questions most often answered themselves from the collective consciousness.

The rarefied energy of these five-day workshops was so intense that even if one of us left for a local Starbucks, our body would feel like it was disintegrating, each of us participants in something greater than any individual attendee.

It was very difficult at times and also the most rewarding work of our lifetime.

Ahhhhh

There was a technique we taught many patients and caregivers called the "Ahhhhh Breath." It worked to relieve tension and on an even deeper level created a remarkable connection between the two participants.

The technique is for one person, perhaps an ailing patient, to lie down on their back so that the person sitting directly beside them can watch the rise and fall of their abdomen. The person lying on the floor needs to do nothing but breathe. The second person sits mid-section next to the first, to closely observe the person's breath in their belly. Focusing on their partner's breath, the person begins to coordinate their respiration with the other's, breathing in when their partner inhales, exhaling as they breathe out. The person sitting up refrains from touching their partner so as not to distract or diffuse the energies. The supine individual's belly naturally rises with each inhalation, and the upright person lets go of their own breath rate so as to take on the other's breath rhythm.

After a few minutes of the two breathing in tandem, each person now sits up, as a common exhale is released, softly makes the sound *Ahhhhh*.

With each exhalation, the one watching the other's breath gently releases the great *Ahhhhh* of letting go. The two connect in an almost spiritual intimacy that builds considerable trust and confidence. In the workshops we recommend that people partner up with someone they don't know just to demonstrate the way the technique can break through the boundaries between each other, between the mind and the heart, allowing healing to cross over the barriers to wellness. One woman, quite delighted with the process, said it was like "crossing the blood barrier between mother and child in-uteri, sharing nutrients and states of mind."

This is a wonderful practice to empower one's children, letting them take the role of sitting up beside the parent and connecting to them with their *Ahhhhh*.

It also works well with one's animals, which we pushed to an extreme one day with an abused Rottweiler named Amma we had rescued. Amma wanted no one near her. If someone passed within six feet, her lips would curl up into a threatening display of her sizable canines, and a threatening growl would warn you off. *Grrrrr* rumbled from the throat of this animal, too battered to trust anyone, warning that she was about to lunge at any passerby, animal or human.

One day I sat down a few feet away, and as she *Grrrrr*ed, I coordinated my out-breath with her display and began to go *Ahhhhh* in tandem with her *Grrrrr*. She was noticeably resistant and a bit confused at what she may have thought was some ruse to do her harm, but I was in no rush and soft of belly just continued my *Ahhhhh* to her *Grrrrr*. A few times a day I would sit with her in her room and *Ahhhhh* to her growl. Soon her *Grrrrr* began to soften into a *Grahhh*. Within the week when I came into the room or passed, she emitted a soft welcoming *Grahhh, grahhh*. Over the next ten years she became one of the most loving and sweetest retired attack dogs we had ever known. We were impressed with how close to the surface even the most heavily armored heart can come when called by love.

The Holy Pizza of Infinite Compassion

After a few months of teaching a weekly class about conscious living and conscious dying at St. Vincent's Hospital in Santa Fe, we were invited to be pastoral care counselors.

It was there that we met a nurse in her fifties, Joanne, who was facing the same cancer as many of the patients she had served. She was a reserved, long-divorced, woman with breast cancer and the additional wound of an eighteen-year-old daughter who had turned away from her. Perhaps acting out against an imagined abandonment, her daughter began to live the low life, which included drugs and alcohol, stolen clothes hanging in her closet, and a man older than her mother waiting for her by the curb. The daughter's anger and verbal abuse stung and profoundly confused Joanne. Most assuredly, the daughter did not want to hear anything about her mother's needs from us.

None of Joanne's coworkers came to visit. She felt they might have an irrational fear of making contact with her breast cancer, but actually she had been so cold toward others that she had made no friends. So there we were, standing where her family and friends might have been, if she had any, which is not an unusual situation for hospice workers to find themselves in.

Indeed, where we live, in an area of large families, often clans, who live in close proximity to each other, we have found that fewer counselors such as ourselves are required, since multiple family members are there to help.

Joanne said she wanted to get out of the hospital and go home, but she had no support group waiting for her; so we told her we would put together a team to help her through what promised to be her final weeks. Ironically, the group we gathered was largely composed of community members of our weekly hospital Conscious Living/Conscious Dying gatherings, many whom discovered that this would become their life's work, as their heart swung toward deep-hearted service.

The group did all the shopping, cooking, laundry, organization of medications, and doctors' visits. Stephen and I were part of her care schedule, and one of us would sleep over at her house when no one else was available.

She had a difficult time with seizures, some physical movements, and verbal confusion, which were the effect of a metastasis in the brain. We gave her a picture of her beloved Jesus (the Self-Realization Fellowship image, being one of our favorites) to look at if she felt a seizure coming on. It seemed to give her comfort until one night, unable to sleep, she took her walker into the living room, and something very odd happened. Light poured from the image of Jesus on the shelf, a light so bright she could read the titles of the books nearby.

When we saw her the next day, after telling us about her experience the previous night, Joanne stood up; she didn't need a walker, her speech was clear, her eyes shone. She had, by her own estimation, been blessed. We laughed that, because she so rarely went to church, Jesus had to come to her. She said she wasn't concerned about anything, all she could feel was Jesus's love.

Knowing from experience that this illumined state might not last, we spoke of how miracles might be reflected in the body of illness. How they might provide a deeper realignment in the heart than a drastic change in the body.

"What would it be like if your body didn't continue to respond with a sense of wholeness, like your heart has?" we asked. "Would you feel as unworthy of God as you once did? Or could you visualize those luminous eyes looking, clarifying, streaming light into your being? Could you breathe in the light and breathe out all the darkness, all the obstacles to loving kindness that obscure the experience of the Beloved?"

Joanne said she felt more loving and loved than she ever had. She was particularly struck by the kindness of strangers who she now felt were her true friends. She never knew such simple acts could be so generous, so able to make her happy.

After "being bathed in that light," she felt she should be baptized again. Rather than allow this wish to increase her old sense of helplessness, we started the process to make it happen. We played with the idea that it might be time for a Baptism–pizza–good-bye party for Joanne and her wonderfully supportive volunteer team who had served and loved her over the last six months. She became quite excited about the idea and, for the week proceeding, asked repeatedly, as her brain was more affected each day, when the party was to be held.

On a Sunday evening, twenty of her closest friends and "helpers" came to form a circle around her and sing what amounted to love songs—"Amazing Grace" and "Jesus on the Mainline." She sang along with her angelic choir, blissed out!

Sharing "The Holy Pizza of Infinite Compassion," we held hands and walked in a slow circle around her, each person entering the circle to hug her and wish her "safe passage," and farewell. Stephen and I stayed for some time after everyone else departed, laughing and singing with Joanne about the joy that even death could be met with when one's heart was open, as she held the picture of Jesus to her heart.

A few weeks after this event, Joanne started having further problems with her brain. Her physician felt it was time for her to go back to the hospital where there were doctors always available. She was getting close to death. When we visited her and sat close so she could hear, she began to arrange her wig to cover the hair she had lost from the chemotherapy. We asked her, "Do you think you are your hair? Do you think Jesus cares a whit how you're dressed? Your heart is so beautiful and He is waiting for you. He wants to wrap His arms around you and take you into the Universal Heart."

She died soon after that last meeting. We weren't with her at the time, as we have found that many people, once they feel the work is finished, prefer to die alone. They are at peace with not having to be polite or protect anyone volunteering or visiting. They just breathe themselves out of their body—it's just the in-breath and out-breath, so natural.

This freedom-propelled departure sometimes leaves loved ones lost in feelings of having let a loved one down, not realizing it was just that the dying person, who was not alone but with the One, had a perfect opportunity to head home.

TEN

A Shared Mind

THOUGH I KNEW HOW to work with dying patients, I had a lot to learn about teaching and meditating, learning how to be a whole human being; to do Buddhist practice without what Stephen called "taking on the Buddha mask."

At my request, over about two years, he put me through "the Buddhist ringer" of level after level of questioning, investigating, and exploring intention, motivation, clarity, and delusion, getting me ready to teach meditation to the groups. He questioned me over and over about the depth of my understanding. I loved to be tested. Particularly by someone who loved me.

I learned to speak differently and use fewer words to say what needed to be said. I had a tough time not repeating myself. I found it very difficult to say exactly what I meant and to be clear. Stephen often rephrased what I was saying in a clearer way. We both got frustrated and laughed at times.

He was teaching me to speak directly from one heart to another, so a student could hear what was being said without feeling judged. It only intensified our bond. We shared our gifts and frailties. I never attempted anything so difficult or so rewarding.

It took me two years to integrate it all and begin imparting skillful means for mediation. I didn't want a free ticket. I wanted to earn my genuine teacher's certificate, so to speak, my "bona fide," to legitimately teach on my own.

As I learned to teach and sat on stage with him, I sent love and encouragement to the participants to forgive themselves and to answer their own questions from whatever love they discovered. I even spoke alone to our growing groups who wanted to know more about my healing process. I became more comfortable watching the audiences judge me—"Who was this person teaching with Stephen?"—and I attempted to stay mindful of the many states of mind that arose. Aware that the more self-conscious I became, the less well my connection with the hearts of others could be maintained. It may have been the first time in my life that I saw how the possibility of letting go of my self-consciousness could be for the benefit of others. To modify the ego for another's well-being was not self-protection but compassion, and that's what motivated me.

Of course, everyone has their own way, but our ways together seemed to fit just right. We were in an exciting learning curve that brought us ever closer, sometimes even in our dreams.

When I had read Elizabeth Kubler-Ross's books many years earlier, I was moved by her life story. It encouraged me to take people deeper to help them "finish their business," which, of course, besides allowing one to have a conscious good-bye to one's life, is also the basis of one's own forgiveness work.

We explained developing a skillful life review process in our book, *A Year to Live*. It aids in the merciful investigation, even the envisioning, of what it might be like to open to death, to surrender blockage after blockage to the heart, the stop-gaps to peace. As the poet Kabir said, "If you don't break your ropes while you're alive, do you think ghosts will do it for you afterward?" Acknowledging what

I already intuitively knew, I saw how much more work needed to be done to fully integrate the mind into the heart.

Stephen's world, even his language, was so different to me. He used common Asian spiritual expressions, shared by his spiritual family, like the word *sadhana* for spiritual and meditation practice. He used the word *sanga* (tribe) for spiritual family; *Dharma* for practice or teaching, truth, or the moment as it is; and *Sukka* for pleasure, or *dukkha* for pain. Unlike most spiritual practitioners, he belonged to two different *sangas*. A Hindu group from which his friend Ram Dass and his teacher Maharaji originated, with whom he had practiced for decades, and a Buddhist *sanga* with whom he taught for even longer, which included his friends and teachers Joseph Goldstein, Sharon Salzberg, and Jack Kornfield, who had long ago suggested that he teach.

He taught me everything he knew. Then I taught him the rest.

One day sitting in the living room I asked him, "When you look across the room, what do you see?" I waited a moment and I said, "Just the wall?!" And quick as he always was, he swooned and said, "Oh no, no, I see the fine rain of energy that fills the space between us and that wall!" He always was a quick learner—the quickest I have ever known.

Our exchanges were some of the fastest growth processes either of us had ever experienced. It was as if we could mention something to one another and it would prime the pump for a considerable unfolding of insight.

My whole life I have had sensory overload reaction to touch, *synesthesia,* which made it difficult for me to be touched. Also, normal sounds became uncomfortably loud. Because of my profoundly dyslexic inclinations, I am easily startled. Even after living 24/7 with Stephen in our little home, he can come around a corner and cause me to *yip* in surprise. He thus learned to announce his presence before entering or passing by saying, "It's me." But now he sings as he enters a room or approaches me from out of sight. Every once in a while, when we simultaneously enter the hall from either end, and I unexpectedly see him, I'll emit my energetic gasp and, he, as I come into view, will in turn get startled and emit an equally audible gasp, as a great gale of laughter drops us both to our knees.

Investigating this pattern has reinforced my sense that it may have been an offshoot of the dyslexia. Though with my early conditioning, it was not out of the question that I might have a little of what's called "untouched monkey" syndrome, it made me become more aware of my body, in general; even the tone of my voice became more fluid. As I softened, some of our long-time retreatants asked what had happened to me since I sounded so different.

I never had any difficulty hugging the sick or dying, but initially embracing strangers was just too intimate. But as I began to open to all the loving hugs that I had stiffened to in the beginning, I became a major hugger, as will be seen in a later story.

We both, for somewhat different reasons, began to show our teeth as our smiles broadened. This was quite different for Stephen, having been taught incorrectly early on from a fundamental Buddhist teacher that true aspirants never showed their teeth when they smiled, and for myself because I was a stone-faced monkey who was taught never to express her feelings.

Because of our growing psychic connection, often sharing each other's thoughts, with laughter and occasional awe, and our devotion to each other, we began to explore the devotional condition known as "mystical union," which later evolved into our book *Embracing the Beloved*.

In the group dynamic, the vague auras I was once so proud and scared of grew to bright neon intensity for both of us. My ego would have spun out of control if I didn't have my meditation practice to give me some insight into the pitfalls that could lie ahead.

Stephen was a quick wit, had a natural sense of humor, and had been active in many interesting spiritual scenes in the course of his dozens of years on the path. He'd been a poet and coordinator of readings at the Gaslight in Greenwich Village, and an editor of the *San Francisco Oracle* in Haight-Ashbury a few years later. Eventually he became a contributor in Buddhist community publications and a co-teacher with his old friend Ram Dass, and his dear friend Elizabeth Kubler-Ross, by whom he was initiated into his now well-known work and writings about death and dying.

Many, it appeared, wanted to be close to him, but somewhat to my surprise, he had, like myself, a natural inclination to live quietly, or as quietly as one could playing with three young children. He has a natural hermit gene and liked the meditative life, to be alone with his work and to have time for his "patients." (We never did find a better word than this; because we did not charge for counseling, the word "clients" did not seem appropriate either.)

He did not have much interest in the social world that sometimes pulled at him. I was a loner because I felt I never fit in; he a loner because he fit in too well and found "the scene" a bit of a distraction. We fit together perfectly.

Part of my practice naturally evolved into being open to strangers in crowded venues such as stores and supermarkets. People would turn to me for no apparent reason and without me saying a word begin to speak to me as if I was something between a psychologist and their very best friend. Even if I unintentionally made eye contact with someone, a little far away, they would come over to me and start telling me about the recent death of a relative or an operation they were considering.

Yesterday in the market a woman came over to me and shared her fears about her parents visiting and all the judgments and confusion that would entail—how her parents would go on about her being overweight. I stopped and softened my belly to be present and open to her needs. She said she would always break out in pimples before they arrived. I told her I felt the same and knew many people whose parents gave them a rash. We laughed a bit together. She said she felt fine about her weight and her husband loved her "as is." That was the beginning of a forty-five minute conversation between the broccoli and the spinach in the frozen food section.

When I first found myself in these situations, I had an abundance of "wise" advice, but now it is more heart than mind that attends to their wounds. I open for their unbinding and don't really have any great wisdom for them, just an acceptance of their/our human condition—a shared heart, perhaps.

Softening the Wounded Healer

One day I was standing in the bedroom and felt a huge weight descend on me. I fell back onto the bed. My mind thundered like an approaching locomotive. I lay there like a boulder in a stream, the approaching sound coming closer and closer. There was no escape, nowhere to run. Surrender was the only way out.

The great sound approaching, the roar of "The Lion of Truth," the one that eats your lies and spits out what remains—all the afflictive emotions, all the guilt, all the lack of forgiveness and self-loathing— and I just had to lie there and stay present and let the steam engine of the mind run over me. My body let go of its history of holding. My gut released. First, my abdomen, then my heart, opened, leaving me soft of belly and with a sense of physical and emotional freedom. There were levels and levels of softening, levels and levels of letting go of feeling after feeling. No fear, no grasping, just the unnamed grace that seems to be the antidote for the unnamed sorrow.

Until this lightness of being showed itself, I never realized how rigidly my abdomen was being held. This moment-to-moment softening of the hardening in the belly directly related to the armor over my heart. Softening the belly, the heart began to melt in waves of gratitude. The body opened . . . the belly softened . . . the heart boundless

. . . mind cleared . . . and there was peace, and that of which peace is an expression.

How slow and painful (to ourselves and others) is the rise through the realms of our hungry ghost. I saw with mercy and awareness, in what now seems like someone else's life, how my trying to hide from pain, to hand it off to religion or astral delights, delayed the discovery of a compassion and clarity that would serve others, as much as myself.

I was becoming comfortable in the role of "wounded healer," a person who learns from their own pain how to be merciful and sensitive to the pain of others. I was learning how to heal the body, mind, and heart torn by unfortunately familiar circumstances. It was a path to dealing with the suffering of others by displaying a mercy that softens my own pain.

In many group meetings we spoke about the escape mechanisms we are encouraged to employ. In the absence of the self-mercy of direct investigation, we can often make things worse. We turn life into an emergency, ignoring the option of softening around pain and instead choose a tightening that turns pain into suffering, intensifying the discomfort.

Quite naturally, in the process of girding for self-protection, our belly steels itself for battle. Our belly guards the old wounds. But sometimes, as much out of exhaustion as self-mercy, we momentarily let go of the rigidity that holds our suffering in place and our belly softens for a moment and we get a glimpse beyond our sorrow.

Thinking we are not up to handling our grief is a form of grief itself. Distrusting ourselves and the process, sometimes our grief misinforms us about our capacity to work with it. Softening to that grief, we find that even when we feel hopeless we are not helpless.

We're not referring to the agony of a crushed hand or broken nose—not even many yogis are capable of staying soft with that—but most ordinary pain, physical and even mental, can be soothed a bit by *moving toward the wound with a merciful awareness* instead of tightening the gut and heading for the first emergency exit.

This is obvious when attending to the pain of another, particularly a loved one. When we meet their discomfort with pity, overcoming our urge to withdraw and be elsewhere, we embrace the pain, turning toward it instead of away from it, "to be there for them."

Some years ago Stephen and I went to one of our teachers and asked how we might get rid of a chronic challenge that often disturbed our meditation. He said, "Don't look for relief; look for the truth." It was reminiscent of one of the great teachers of old who, when asked by a student how to get rid of a painful situation in their life, said, "I don't come to answer your questions; I come to heal them!"

We are all wounded minds seeking the healing we have taken birth for. We are all healers on the way toward completion, and by tending to our lives with mercy and awareness, we serve the pain we all share.

The teaching of *soft belly* aids many working with physical and mental discomforts by building a safe haven in which to explore hidden resources when there sometimes seems no end of difficulty. It gives us space in which to process afflictive emotions.

Sometimes, a shield is found across the abdomen which mirrors the armoring over the heart. It is the ache of impermanence and the remnants of fear and helplessness, often buried there over a lifetime. It's not about opposing the hardness, but about meeting it with a soft mercy, knowing we cannot let go of anything we do not accept.

One afternoon, after a long meditation, at a retreat in Eureka, California, I opened my eyes and said to Stephen, "You won't believe what I just heard. I heard a woman's soft, sweet voice. I knew at once it was the Mother of Mercy, Kuan Yin, Mother Mary, saying, 'My arms are always around you; all you have to do is put your head on my shoulder.'"

I was just amazed, particularly because of my relationship to "mother," I could hear a mother's voice filled with love and acceptance.

How long I had longed for that! We cried. It changed my relationship from "my mother" to "the Mother."

Eureka indeed!

Getting Playful

Because Stephen and I are so similar in so many ways, some of the descriptions he used of his experiences apply remarkably to mine. An example of the quality of heart-to-heart transmission displayed itself one day when he was returning home from teaching with the Zen Master Seung Sahn (also known as San Sa Nim), in a rather rarefied state. Though I don't recall all that he told me about their exchange, I remember that the absolute joy and freedom of their interchange was causing him to glow.

During their lunch break Stephen had asked Seung Sahn, "Please teach me about koans." Koans are a Zen means of peeling back level after level of mind by use of a spiritual "riddle" which has no apparent logic, but reveals a supra-rational intuitive answer. Seung Sahn smiled the smile of someone waiting for precisely that question and began the first koan with these few words: "no expectation" and "present only" and "just go straight," offering a mind-dispelling conundrum.

Stephen had always been "Mr. Wisdom," quick to reply to the confusion of others, but this time it was his confusion, and the ground grew unsteady beneath him.

After a few hesitant, faulty replies mimicking back some aspect of the question which seemed to have no rational answer, Seung Sahn tapped him on the shoulder and said, "Don't be attached to the words of the Zen Master." And as irrational as the nature of the questions themselves were, something opened, and they both started "popping koans" one after another. Stephen said he had never laughed so hard in his life. The two of them were like jazz musicians, trading fours.

Thoroughly nurtured, even without eating lunch, Stephen returned to the meeting room to complete the afternoon's teachings.

A few hours later, playing the perfect Zen Master, just as Stephen was about to answer a question from a participant, Seung Sahn slammed his Zen stick down hard on the dais they were sharing, causing many in the audience to jump, looking over at Stephen, who casually yawned and quite unruffled continued to answer the participant's question, brushing off the attempt to startle him in an act of the "dharma combat" they'd been discussing. Afterward San Sa Nim invited Stephen to teach with him in Europe.

Stephen started sharing the koans that had been presented to him, and after showing me how and where the answers could be found in the space between thoughts, I started to laugh and began "answering," quite to my amazement, one koan after another. In a matter of minutes the quality of clear mind, imparted by their meeting, was fully ensconced in me as well. Stephen had not taught me *where*, but *how* to find a response. There had been a transmission of the nature of the process, like learning from a dream that had shown me the way. Whatever I had feared in "mysterious Zen" was now like a knock-knock joke, and there was nobody there. It was a most enjoyable experience. The next time Stephen went to teach, Seung Sahn invited me along.

This potential for startling clarity directly transmitted from one being to another—as Seung Sahn had done with Stephen, and Stephen with me—is an example of the shared consciousness of the unimpeded heart, the essence of spiritual friendship.

✳

A game we used to play lying in bed before going to sleep was called "three-word tales." One of us would give the other three words around which to contrive something akin to a bedtime story. He would say, "monkey, tulip, floorboard," and I would weave a monkey story perhaps about finding out that the monkey had a broken floorboard through which a tulip had appeared, and the travails he went through to find another yellow and blue flower to keep it company since it was able to grow indoors without need of the sun, thriving only on the monkey's rapt attention and wholehearted admiration of its beauty, on and on.

At first my stories were only a few sentences long, as I was not confident in this free-wheeling use of my imagination or ability to make acrobatic characters out of dyslexic heavy-footedness. But soon this exquisite bonding exercise drew paragraphs and ten-minute-long fairy tales—even cloud sutras that fed our hearts and dreams.

The other evening, just to make the game as difficult as possible, and to be able to watch his bright-mindedness unfold, I said to Stephen, "pig's feet, rock fall, tiger trap." After he stopped laughing, he told me the story of the Bodhisattva pig who saved a tiger who was about to eat him when the tiger slipped into a hunter's animal catch pit. Instead of running away, the pig calmed the great tiger and began pulling rocks and dirt into the pit to form some sort of escape ramp so that the tiger could climb out. The pig continued until he wore away his tender hooves creating a sloping rock fall by which the tiger could climb to safety. The grateful tiger, instead of eating him, knowing that because the pig had worn out his feet he could no longer forage for himself, brought him food so he would not starve. But when the tiger brought the pig a rabbit or a piece of deer leg, the pig told him he only ate vegetables and that he felt better if he did not kill anything as it was against his precepts to cause unnecessary harm to anyone or anything. The pig was quite satisfied with a big, shiny banana leaf rolled full of fresh roots and tender barks, fruit pickings and shelled nuts, in what they called a "jungle burrito." Inspired by the pig, the tiger became a vegetarian too and taught the gorillas and the panda bears as well not to eat other animals anymore. And that is why, to this day, gorillas and pandas are vegetarians, who only mainly eat plants and leaves. Or so it went during one of our impromptu bedtime stories.

One day Stephen turned to me in the living room and asked me if he could put his head in my lap because he was "going through something." He said, "I can see past the edge of the Universe from here."

This was no ordinary meditation but a considerably more potent upwelling. He was having a spontaneous *kundalini* experience in which sizable amounts of energy are released in the body, traveling through the heart in substantial waves of love and compassion which continue through a powerfully lucid mind, out the top of the head, to share such miraculous blessings with the multi-leveled universe.

Perhaps, it has been postulated, these long-recorded historic events of the spontaneous unfolding of luminosity called *kundalini* in the yogic framework (and simply "grace" in so many other belief systems) are indeed the origin in early man of the conviction that there is a good deal more to us than what we think, feel, or even know—a primal release of inherent "spiritual energy" and the abilities it germinates, the "strong medicine" shamans say presage healing abilities.

St. Paul, mothers in childbirth, those at the edge of death, even astronauts in the indescribable vastness of space—all occasionally speak of experiencing such alterations in perception, which create other remarkable realities. Each recognized their vision from a different point of view and related it as such: some saw angels descending to bless them, others saw those same angels rolling the rock back from the mouth of the cave to allow a returned Jesus to pass. Seeing the deathlessness, most were never quite so afraid thereafter.

I admit I was slightly jealous of this most familiar gift from on high, or more accurately from deep within, and I told Stephen that he had gotten a golden ticket and should enjoy the precious ride!

I was pleased that Stephen so honored the experience which I had found so valuable when I was younger. Though at that time I imagined I was going nuts, I nonetheless knew from that point on that death was just a superstition which made us small, while love could carry us well beyond ourselves.

Sometime after this experience, something similar to my own psychic seeing began happening to Stephen. He began to see something like auras, not quite haloed colors around people, but the people themselves, "turned a kind-of-a sherbet color." Their hands and faces became a soft, shining purple, red, or green or occasionally black. He experimented with it to see if those who displayed a black or charcoal color might signify that they were going to die. But it did not.

Because this phenomenon tended to happen later in the day, we imagined it might have been the result of personal purification as compassion displaced mercilessness, ridding the body/mind of toxins. What was going on in those events was alchemical.

Shaman's Song

Sometimes from our densest shadows come the most useful illuminations. Or, to clarify the subject, sometimes in the heavily guarded shadows, light is allowed to enter for the benefit of others. Having gradually emerged from my early conditioning not to touch, perish the thought, and not to hug, came a call from my pain. To take it in my arms.

I was never quite sure what more I could offer than my support and practical commentary at a ten-day Conscious Living/Conscious Dying retreat, when someone asked me if I would simply hold her. Off in a corner we sat on the floor, and I held her for some time like I would hold a frightened child. She couldn't stop crying, she was releasing, and I couldn't ignore the continued awakening in my own heart.

This was the beginning of a new addition to the healing techniques we shared at the gatherings, which I organically began to offer to the group. Soon after lunch break, whoever wished to join me could be hugged in silence, in a separate room. By the time I got to the room, a dozen people were waiting. At first, it seemed I would have enough time to hold everyone. However, after hugging the first person, when I came out to invite the next one in, the line had grown to a couple dozen more folks. Seeing we would need a little organization to pull this thing off, we instituted the process that after someone was in with me for fifteen minutes, the next person in line would ring a bell and enter after the other left. It was not unlike the melting faces, which come for penance, and healing that I saw before I fell asleep each night.

One after another sat next to me and just slipped into my arms. Nothing needed to be said. We just looked into each other's eyes and shared the common sadness. I needed only to love; they needed only to be loved.

Sometimes I picked up the origin of their painful thoughts, but words would only have diminished our connection. When our minutes were over I sometimes told them I loved them just as they were or that they were forgiven for anything they had ever done to hurt themselves or another. The line grew so quickly that the first session lasted ten hours. The next day was the same.

When I got back to our room, well into the evening, Stephen asked me if I had just taken a shower because my hair was so wet. He was nearly ecstatic when I told him I hadn't taken a shower, that my hair was soaked with tears.

After that, the well-intended organization of the "grief line" broke down and people would just come up to me wherever we were, at lunch, in breaks, in the bathroom, and throw their arms around me and begin to cry. By the time the workshop was over, there were still people waiting to be held. I told them we were very fatigued but I would try, at the next retreat, and keep them in my meditations in the meantime. I felt badly that we had to leave, as this was a true gift to me, as apparently, it was to others.

It was clear that love was the only gift worth giving.

When I was hugging so many wounded people in the retreats and seeing something quite wonderful as a result of simply transmitting love, it reminded me of the various contacts we had with native healers. I certainly am no shaman, but sometimes I feel that same quality of energy when we are working with those deprived of mercy in their lives, those, perhaps, whose shame bears down on their illness. There is a natural warmth from which this energy arises, which is drawn toward healing. It is called forth directly from the source, from prayers and meditations, contemplations, and a great need for compassion. We have met those whose long purifications have brought forth what is called "a healing song." Sometimes you can hear the song; sometimes you can only feel it.

Their spirit energy comes from clearing the hindrances to their natural light and sharing their radiance through their voice and hands. It allows them, during spirit travels, to reach outward, through the realms beyond birth and death to be able to focus their energy like a laser beam on what opens to it. They collaborate with the spirits, whose nature is well beyond ordinary understanding.

They can send healing dreams from the ground of their being, on which it is said their ancestral spirits walk, and they wait to receive the echo. They do not call this a conduit from the "other world," but their own gift to be shared.

Their song is a bridge across the broken heart; drawing from the source of healing, residing in each cell, a release of the soul.

The shaman's song reminds me of the earth beneath my feet, the boundless sky of the mind, and the radiant sun of our heart. It reminds me to complete my birth.

> *The coyote women were talking in the woods last night.*
> *They seemed lonely and excited.*
> *Before I met Stephen, unhappy,*
> *I thought they were complaining about their mates.*
> *Now it seems they speak only of the Beloved.*

ELEVEN

Is This That?

YEARS LATER, WE INSTALLED a twenty-four-hour "Grief Hot-line," as coordinators of the Hanuman Foundation Dying Project. We were often on the phone for eight to ten hours a day, especially after *Psychology Today* did a feature on our work from which we received three hundred letters and eight hundred phone calls, which took us months to respond to.

Though I worked with several people in the final chapter of their life, until the grief hotline I had never been confronted with so many, with such immediate needs. I was learning to listen from a different space. I wasn't always checking my defenses, receiving others in a non-judgmental stillness; the heart had room for everything, hearing them deeply enough so that they could hear themselves. They were met by a healing kindness that encouraged them to attend to their unfinished business—to release their innermost thoughts and feelings to a complete stranger. I virtually took their hand and walked with them into the fears and hopes, the submerged states of mind, that many had so painfully and skillfully eluded. Gradually, I was able to enter the pain and healing with them, side-by-side in a healing pilgrimage.

Working on the book *Embracing the Beloved,* our desks and karma touching, Stephen and I often shared aloud in a remarkable harmonic the insights we sought to express in some ongoing chapter. Sometimes Stephen was so rapturous that when he typed it was almost as though he was playing a concert piano. His hands rose, his wrists became like ocean waves, his fingertips descended on the keys, ecstatic harmonies falling to the page. Sometimes, he would hesitate just for a moment, his hands suspended in midair, a word eluding him just before it came instead into to my mind, as I interjected some phrase and the music went on. Our luckiest days, when we were most attuned to the subject and each other, were the high point of our collaboration. We have worked like this on many books over the past thirty-seven years. Sometimes our connection leaves us breathless.

In our first few years together there was, of course, the play of bodies and minds introducing themselves on level after level, while discovering each other and themselves in the bargain. Lesser/old ways auditioned and were dismissed. But even in the times when our minds were clouded, beyond the confusion was the ever-present palpable interconnectedness and commitment that reminded us to enter together the heart of healing. At times, it was hard to tell if we were pilgrims on the path or clowns in the circus, but the next step was always the same: to let go into love. It was mercy deepening from moment-to-moment, awareness unstuck from its object, we put down our load as we were able, slowly exorcizing the ghosts of unfinished business with the past. Healing.

The potential of a healing relationship is in its ability to triangulate on the "mystery" with an openness of mind that no longer clings to the "known," and a heart vulnerable to the truth.

High End of a Curve

The phenomenon that most separates couples or members of any group is perception—how we see, hear, feel, experience, and interpret objects in our sensory fields. How we see affects what we see. This is why in court trials at times "eyewitness" testimony is considered unreliable. One person sees a gun in a passerby's hand, and another sees a banana, while a third may see a cell phone. There is a lifetime of decoding that occurs in a microsecond of recognition and identification. What we see depends on our expectations and what we have previously experienced.

To recognize how we perceive brings considerable insight. The bioelectricals that transmit perceptions from the eye to the brain do not carry an exact replica of what has been received; rather they synthesize a chemical equivalency which, it turns out, mimics powerful hallucinogens, causing the mind to not so much recognize what is being experienced as, in a manner of speaking, hallucinate it. In other words, we don't so much see what's coming in over the wire as dream it.

"Is it the same or different?" the Roshi quietly asks, elucidating that on one level everything is different and on another everything is the same. Each person differs by what makes them happy, yet everyone is similar in the essential desire for happiness.

Our choices are our karma. What has gone before articulates what is to come: what we want, cling to, or attempt to elude, resist, and escape from. Perception reflects the history of our experiences guided by the satisfying or unpleasant result of previous conditioning. There is little that is just as it seems.

I cannot make any decision because, as the saying goes, I am of two minds about it. Observing any situation, any state of mind, there is often an equal and an opposite, both valid, condition mirrored in consciousness. On some days I might make people uncomfortable because I took no stance, told no stories, proffered no attitude, which apparently didn't satisfy their desire to be cosmetically mirrored or acknowledged, have an opinion, or offer a choice. Conversely when I did opine, I could make the same people just as uncomfortable. When intuition moves me, without intention, when thoughts think themselves in the vastness, they become just objects floating in space, identical.

It is at these times, when my heart dictates the next step, when I offer my life to healing, that I most regale. I don't so much analyze what to do next or which way to turn, as I become an innocent bystander, observing the intuition at the wheel, happy to be so near my axis.

It's not as if in those two conflicting minds that one says yes and the other no. They both say yes! I can see just about everyone's point of view. Even if I don't agree with them, their logic is nonetheless evident. I'm not one to drive a waiter or waitress crazy waiting for me to make up my mind. Anything is pretty much as good as anything else. And the deeper I go, the less definable I become, and the more real. I think I might do one thing under a certain circumstance, but then surprise myself by doing quite the opposite. And it is often better, as long as it doesn't lose its ground or get too cerebral to contain the simple truth. Stephen once said I was a buried treasure.

One day, the man delivering propane to the house, while kneeling down to show me how to check the pipes for a leak, reached under my skirt and touched me. He was a dead man! My formidable dog, an Akita, extremely attentive to my moods, needed only hear a frightened or angry change in my tone to approach with teeth bared, and our timber wolf would not have been far behind.

Because mindfulness gives us a long moment to consider our next move, rather than automatically react, I was able to respond in a millisecond of mercy that disconnected what might be called "the trigger mechanism." Keeping my voice calm, I scolded him instead of making this a very bad day for him. Having worked with so many women who have been raped, I always imagined that if someone touched me that way I would bring considerable misery down on his head. But to my surprise what came through me was a measured (just to keep him alive), stern voice that a mother who knew her child had done something very, very wrong might use.

"How could you of all people do this? You have a mother. What would you feel if someone did this to your mother? You were not taught to act so badly. What would God think of your actions? You better go to confession right now and ask for forgiveness. You better get out of here while the getting's good and think about what you just did."

He began to cry and said he didn't know why he would do such a terrible thing to me. The wolf nudged closer, the Rottweilers came up from downstairs; my four canine guardians waiting for a signal, wondering if everything was okay. I told the delivery man to get out and never come back.

We knew his boss well but didn't say anything because we knew this fellow had a wife and children, and it would have been impossible for him to get another job in this area if word got out. It was my intention, as I distinctly imprinted on him, my finger to his chest, that if I ever heard word of such doings from any of the neighbors, he would be out of a job and into prison.

Concerned that other women in the community might have suffered the same improper touch, I asked around but heard nothing bad about him. I attributed his action to recently having lost a young child. This, of course, is no excuse but it was a motivation for us to send a healing meditation his way, while nonetheless staying attentive to any whisper of bad acts on his part.

It was interesting to me that I responded so differently than I ever would have imagined. If I had not been so well protected and had such latitude for action, I might have picked up a bottle and broken it over his head. But that precious millisecond of choice to respond rather than react, cultivated by years of mindfulness practice, offered unrecognizable possibilities. If I had automatically reacted with a swift intervention to his unseemly act, no one would have blamed me! When passing us on the road, he now hangs his head, as if asking for forgiveness. No other events, as far as we have heard, have occurred in the last ten years.

And the mind on the high end of a curve, allows mindfulness to make the decisions, and opens brightly in the dusk.

Who Is This That Thinks Herself the Ego?

Ego is another name for the do-it-yourself mental construct we call "I," a hand-built Hobbit house of praise or blame, joy or shame, addicted to the feedback its essential emptiness elicits from the environment.

We say "I am" as a declaration that we exist, but we give all that very little credence as we dedicate most of our resources to the polishing of the "I" and almost no attention to the investigation of the "amness." It is *amness* which took birth before the "I" put on the guise of some social identity.

It is said the Buddha only used the word "I" as a convenience. The homemade concept "I" is constantly changing, continuously referring to itself as something more appealing than it is; while this *amness* which animates us—the living suchness we are told by the greatest spiritual masters from Jesus, to Mother Mary, to Buddha and Kuan Yin never dies—is really the best of us.

As I relate directly to the essential state of *amness*, this boundaryless spaciousness of being that contains everything including the floating fallacy of the common "I," the easier it is to fit in my skin. *Amness* is the origin of the treasure in the seven billion of us, fumbling to prove we are worthy of survival.

My process was not to indulge my every whim but instead to call myself out of the shadows and approach illness with warmth and clarity. To embrace with mercy and awareness that which I had alternately ordained and condemned. To simply observe, making as few waves as possible on the Reservoir of Grief, the self-interest in my ordinary thoughts.

It's like that old story about the Sufi rascal Nasruddin who goes into a bank to cash a check and the teller, not knowing who this shabby-looking fellow is, asks for identification. To which Nasruddin pulls out a little mirror, and looking into it, says, "Yup, that's me all right!"

Big surprise! The flat cartoon of "I" that is full of becoming, that imagines itself more this than That, misses completely the absolute joy of just being in pure *amness*.

Some years ago, we went to an ophthalmologist for an eye checkup. He was an old friend whose office was in a hospital where we had done a few in-services talks, so it was quite a normal and rather playful visit. My eyes checked out fine, and as the last procedure, when the usual eye-dilatation drops were put in my eyes, the doctor said I would not be able to see very clearly for a few hours. And he added that I would, of course, not be able to drive or read until my eyes returned to normal.

After he put in the drops, I told him I would be fine to drive because I had never seen so clearly. Whatever the drops did, they removed from my vision the rain of energy I normally had to look through. The doctor thought I was kidding, but being familiar with my peculiarities, he asked me to read the eye chart on the wall. I read the smallest print on the bottom line without difficulty. The doctor, having been to a few of our workshops and being a devotional type himself, started to bow to me. He told us he never met anyone who could see clearly through these diagnostic chemicals.

I didn't think much of it, but when the drops wore off, I got my normal energy seeing back again. The doctor wept. An unintended effect of the mystery.

The Eater of Impurities

For years we sat with people who were dying and listened to stories of complicated lives and the entanglements that actions devoid of kindness had carved into their bones, killing their cells one after another, until there was almost nothing left of them to die or remain alive.

Over the years, one level of our work was most characterized by the exercise called "The Eater of Impurities" we did at a few retreats. This old Native American practice was often done on the solstice.

People sat in a big circle at one end of a meadow, and "the Eater" would sit quietly at the other. Each person would approach, well out of the hearing of the others, and divulge a long-held secret pain, some hidden hindrance to their heart. They would often come with their head slightly down, and sit without preamble or excuse, simply saying those words that perhaps were never uttered before. They would approach me or Stephen acting as "Eater," and we would say to them, "Give it to me," and whatever secrets had caused them or others pain would tumble out.

Much of the material that was shared was common sexual secrets that had separated them from others for much of their lives. Secrets which they felt were unique to themselves but were so often shared by the person before them and the dozen that followed. Some might share a childhood miscreancy which had made another's life more difficult or an unintended, unmindful action that had betrayed another. Or lying and stealing that had grown in proportion over the years. One woman spoke to me of cheating on her husband. Her husband told Stephen he was cheating on his wife. Some spoke of the pain in their chest because of an unshakable anger for past injustices. These were no small pains held as secrets. It was the expanding arch of mercilessness with others and oneself.

Those who brought their pain to "the Eater" were summarily forgiven for anything they did intentionally or unintentionally. Each was told that the Buddha said they could look the whole world over and not find anyone more deserving of love than themselves.

A few said they felt they had lost the way to their heart and feared they would never find their way back. But with the admission of their secret pain, they felt relieved and that they might not only be able to forgive themselves but to actually pass that mercy on to others.

There were, of course, many different degrees of pain given us to "eat," which were sometimes later shared when the group was in session. For too many, it was the need to have someone help carry the agonizing grief of being the target of childhood sexual abuse, or the loss of dying children.

Blessedly, most had to do with the more general personal missteps of coins stolen from their mother's purse, the prophylactics pilfered from their dad, or the prescription drugs pocketed from the family medicine cabinet. Not to mention the blame laden on siblings for forbidden deeds actually done by the confessor.

One woman brought her secret into the group by blurting out in great shame, "Sometimes when my child is driving me to distraction, I just want to throw him out the window!" She was bent and exhausted by those few words and felt completely isolated from what she imagined were the pure hearts around her. When we asked the group, "How many in the room have felt the same?" a hundred hands went up, and a roar of blessed laughter filled the room, sweeping debris from her heart.

All the shared secrets about petty grievances long barnacled to the heart, all the lies and betrayals, all the times when the heart could not yet see brought the group together in the unexpected possibility of mercy for ourselves and each other.

Listening to these gifts of trust that only compassion could adequately respond to, we moved from *the* pain to *the* love. Each of us coming as close as we might to what the Sufis call "The Open Secret," the ever-available Presence in presence. As one of our teachers said, "When you see with the heart, you see no impurities; you only see the heart."

There is another teaching in this practice that many therapists and counselors and confessors know well. It is the power of the listener to hold a secret in the silent center, and allow it to remain unspoken, comforting all the other secrets there entrusted, securing in the heart all the stories and feelings overheard or given in confidence, empowering the mind.

Sharing confidences can weaken the mind and causes the heart to distrust itself. One means of limiting the sad-innate tendency to gossip is to notice when we are telling someone else's story, to watch our motivation for speaking.

It is not that Stephen and I haven't gossiped to each other, but we have watched this mind-state and noted how painfully it can insult the heart. It never brings us closer to the truth. It never brings more kindness into our lives.

Simply Noting

Our homesickness for our true nature pre-exists our birth. We take birth to discover the Inseparable, in the painful midst of the separate.

We are born with a buried longing for completion, a yearning to experience our great nature. All our clumsy attempts to fulfill desire are a reflection of that longing.

When awareness directly meets itself, through meditation, prayer, or spiritual lightning, we become fully conscious. We discover that what we have been looking for all our lives is what is looking. It is the whole of us. When consciousness becomes more than a mere reflection of awareness bouncing from one object to another, the Beloved throws her blanket over us and we are absorbed in love.

The heart has room for even the personality we have been dealt. As a mindful awareness develops, it becomes clear that we are not the personality, that the personality is a remnant of a long-debated prehistory, a coping mechanism, a mask, through which to face the world, the skeleton of inclinations on which the mind and body are hung.

So, we try to "become enlightened," to change our personality, or at least move it from darker to lighter aspects. But even enlightenment, even perfecting the point of view, does not apparently perfect the personality. We asked His Holiness the Dalai Lama, being suitably respectful, if he ever experienced fear. To which he replied, "Not only do I experience fear, I experience anxiety." When liberation, rather than perfection, is what we seek, a loving mind, the ultimate form of nonresistance, allows anxiety to be observed through a merciful awareness. A very different state of mind arises when we relate *from* anxiety, in which the whole world poses a threat, and relate *to* anxiety, in which even such seemingly unworkable states become an achievement in liberation instead of a defeat.

When we begin to meet the overripe fruits of our personality, the reaction is "big surprise—anger," "big surprise—fear," "big surprise—self-interest again." Then the biggest surprise is that clarity and mercy start to become a habit. And then it's no surprise that even the afflictive states have room to outgrow themselves. To go to pieces in the most constructive sense is to reassemble in the compassionate landscape, reminding ourselves of the possibility of liberation from pain before it turns to suffering.

The Love Song of Those Afloat in That

There is a song in us
that is more than our song.
It rises from the origin of things from which the music never ends
I find you there time and time again
I follow the flute to your door.

Cooking cabbage and dancing with the cat our life simmers on a front burner.
When I told him I had put angels in the pudding he
exchanged his metallic utensil for a big wooden spoon.
We sing to ourselves and the food as we cook. It is one of our happiest practices.
What began as almost an apology to the food gradually became a blessing song,
teachings from broccoli and beans.

When the singing recedes and the chewing begins, their life passes into ours, the eater
and the eaten, like the cooks themselves, come closer to the One.
Planting apples in Eden, the fog rolls through the forest in my dreams.

Curled asleep beside the dogs you enter from stage left,
Buddha's flower in your hand, a slight fandango in the brainpan.

And waking, we're so pleased it's not a dream.

We travel alone our whole lives. It is such grace to share that loneliness with another.

There is a path in the woods which opens onto a green clearing.
There are bear scats there and lion tracks and pools cradled in the rocks where we go
for a cool drink from Buddha's belly.

In the forests we are green, on the mountain we are sky—
the sacred everywhere we turn and turn again.

Each time we remember Jesus, forty days wandering in the heart, Buddha peering
from coyote eyes, we resonate again,
there, in each other's eternity.

I marvel at the ability of consciousness to observe itself. The grace of our capacity to cultivate a liberating awareness, the soul of mindfulness to witness our life with kindness and clarity. Not lost in the commentary which floats by on the stream of consciousness. Simply noting, as one teacher said, the "other voices from other rooms." Letting go of the irretrievable past and the unpredictable future.

Mindfulness is knowing what we are doing while we are doing it, our life not an afterthought but a living presence. Sensation after sensation, thought after thought blowing across the vastness of awareness. Watching how easily we slip into old dreams and forget.

The more aware we are, the closer we are to love.

When the cold indifference with which we attempt to freeze our pain begins to melt, the heart becomes more fully alive. Not hopping from one thought to the next without knowing what we are thinking. Watching the process of thought rather than becoming ensnared in its content.

And when the awareness from which consciousness is created turns toward itself, when consciousness becomes conscious of itself, we get a glimpse of the origin of Creation. We recognize the light behind the shadow-play of consciousness. The wisdom eye, the eye of beauty, opens and our life more gently unfolds.

TWELVE

Advanced Teachings

In 2005, WAKING TO months of mounting aches and pains and hair loss, I went to a local doctor for a trained eye and some blood tests. The next week he called and said Stephen and I should come down to look at the results. Something in his voice had a familiar tone.

At the office he told me my tests revealed some sort of connective tissue immune disorder. This was not a great surprise, since my mother and her sister both had the lupus gene and my aunt had died from it. Oh well, here we go again!

The doctor said my white cell blood count was suspiciously elevated, and that we better get it checked out by a friend of his at a nearby clinic. He called ahead and made an appointment for us. He gave us his doctor friend's name and address and asked us to let him know how everything worked out. A month later, expecting to meet a hematologist, we turned the corner and much to our sad surprise we saw in bold letters on the side of the building Santa Fe Cancer Center.

A shiver went through my body, dislodging whatever denial was behind my strong façade. And just to set this feeling in concrete, at the front doors a patient exiting the building said, "Good luck," as we entered. Inside, another couple leaving through the double glass doors blessed us as well. Clearly this was serious business!

When I received the diagnosis of leukemia, I was disoriented by the fact that this could happen again. But when I allowed the news to settle in, I found I could follow the tightness, the resistance, as it tried to take up residence in my body. I related *to* it rather than *from* it, investigating its body pattern, and how the sensations congregated around certain areas. The legs remembered aching with hope, being thwarted from escape, then remembering too to soften, opening to the sensations, allowing mercy to enter where fear might have tightened like a fist. And I heard myself say, from the heart to the body, "May I get the most out of this possible." This was to be another apprenticeship.

I scared myself silly. Stressing out with fear, I rummaged through the books about healing in our considerable library, which, cold comfort, were donated to us by patients who had died.

I watched states of mind come and go on advancing waves. And I watched the body try to find a place to hide. At first so surprised that I had yet another round of cancer to go through, I knew better than to be surprised. As we used to say to groups in our workshops, "Understanding is not enough." And understanding does not quite reach where this second cancer experience was about to take me.

It was months before my meditation fully touched ground.

I had to forgive the body for betraying me. I had to send compassion into the explosion of cells in my marrow. When one has most forms of cancer, healing energy can be focused in a single tumor or grouping thereof, but with diseases that roam the blood current (as metastases do), one has to broaden the focus to embrace the whole body.

I took every possible supplement until I was taking over 200 pills a day. I had acupuncture, infusions of vitamins and minerals, and other body-balancing elixirs. I submerged myself in an ocean of qigong energy.

Though this cancer was detected only eleven years ago (as of this writing), the doctors think that it had already been eleven years into the process. Indeed it is quite possible that I contracted the illness from the smoke that blanketed us from the 2000 fires at the Los Alamos Laboratories, thirty-five miles downwind.

Another of my doctors concurred, having evacuated the area when surrounded by the smoke from the burning "supposedly covered nuclear waste ponds." Perhaps even more pernicious was the cyanide and other agents in the clouds of red fire retardant that were dropped into the smoke. Stephen may have developed a neurological degenerative condition from this as well. Some professionals we know, after treating burn victims, including most of the local hospital's staff, left the area until the smoke dissipated.

During the first year after my diagnosis, I received eight chemotherapy treatments with the monoclonal antibody Rituxan. There followed about a year of partial remission, and after its effects seemed to be diminishing, I received another eight infusions and experienced a more complete remission, which lasted another year. After which the cancer returned.

The doctors said that because my type of leukemia can work its way through the body quite slowly, I might have several more years to live. Unless the flu or an infection (particularly in the lungs) ends the process right here. It was not possible to give me a "due date."

I watched the fear slowly retreat. I felt an increasing trust in the process. I could hear again. I didn't need to change my diet as most recommend, giving greater support to the immune system, because I already was a vegan. I wanted to exercise more, but I was already walking the dogs an hour and a half through our bright forest. I got a stationary exercise machine, what I called a "Zen bike" because it took me nowhere. I increased my meditation time, and since it is so often said that our intentions do all the work, I increased my intention time as well. I knew my condition was serious, but I felt it was workable.

I spent a lot of time studying, talking with doctors we knew, and turning doctors on to advanced, alternative methods for maintaining health like *The China Study*, after which the doctor himself became a vegetarian. As I read through some of the European medical abstracts and suggested a couple of treatments the doctor felt were worth trying, he called me his "research assistant" when he introduced me to others at the clinic.

Then, higher blood counts and additional evolving markers made me seek more distant assistance. After more tests at a prestigious teaching/research hospital heavily funded by pharmaceutical grants, a "world expert" doctor told me that unless I signed up for his current drug trial, there was "nothing that could be done for me." Apparently, I was a dead woman if I did not take on his new, untested regimen.

I sought another opinion. But the second doctor was in such awe of the world-famous first physician that he blindly agreed with him. Some of the scientists we knew strongly recommended we not stop there but go to another expert who was a Western medical leukemia specialist who had considerable faith in supportive alternative treatments.

It was a very different story at this other world-famous institution, a place where both healing and cure were taken into consideration, where tests were done and redone, and specialists conferred with each other about how long and with what particular considerations my life might best continue forward.

I had begun to wonder if there really was such a thing as an "expert," in that they so often disagreed and seemed so poorly informed as to what even the medical journals had to report. We have a doctor friend who, when diagnosed with an illness, went to four of the world's leading experts to ask what might be the best course of treatment. All four disagreed. It was an unholy war.

I don't mean to turn anyone away from getting treatments, but by becoming better informed, we gain greater insight into what is available and can better consider the suggestions of our physicians and the treatments they assure us will be best for us.

Having worked with many doctors and treatment centers in the course of our thirty-seven years of counseling and support of those in the throes of serious illness, we have observed how some doctors "take it personal" when other medical people are consulted about diagnosis and treatment potentials.

How often, even with the best of intentions, the moldy-old ego (gets that way when we don't shine any light on it) suffers from abandonment issues and can actually "need" to be agreed with. On a few occasions I have seen this to be detrimental to the patient.

Stephen speaks of working as a counselor in a large San Francisco hospital many years ago where there was an oncologist who bragged he never lost a patient to cancer. The nurses' jaws clenched when he said that, and they told Stephen that was because all his advanced patients died from an overprescribed toxic excess of chemotherapy. It was his loss, rather than the patients', that most concerned him.

I came back from the hospital with a greater sense of urgency than when I left. I joined a number of online leukemia blogs seeking insight into others' experience with this illness, sharing my emotional-laden state of mind, to get some feedback. Most shared my concerns, and their own, at various stages of the process. Some were newly diagnosed while others were well along in a great variety of treatments and held momentary hopes or long disappointments. It was confusing, but at least I didn't feel isolated.

Most of those who responded were very supportive, and I recommend the well-known leukemia blogs for information and kindness.

Love in Action

I think the most outstanding teaching from our years of working with illness and grief in ourselves and others was the power of love to bring harmony to a place of imbalance. Learning to send love into mental imbalances and afflictive emotions such as fear, doubt, and self-judgment which tend to defend illness rather than offer healing, directing mercy and even forgiveness to our long conditioned self-rejection, turns the tables on the conviction that we deserve to suffer. How very unkind we can be to ourselves.

Pain met by fear, causing us to retreat from our responsibility, creates a self-pity that leaves us broken and haggard by the side of the road. Pain met by mercy breeds compassion. Self-pity reinforces our duality, our sense of hopelessness and helplessness, separating us from the heart of the matter, weakening the body's trust in healing. Love connects us to our healing.

The gift in the wound that illness provides is to remind the heart to move toward difficulties rather than turn away from them.

For me, this has been a lifelong teaching. I began at ten, with scarlet fever. A year later I was confronted with a rheumatic heart. Then, the profoundly scrambled composite that we came to call a "dervishing dyslexia" both in reading and, less recognized by many, a tumbling of speech and hearing that resulted in a "social dyslexia" as well. I was a laundry list of attention-twisting symptoms. Also in the mix of what Stephen called my "initiation" was cancer in my twenties and again at age fifty-nine, a diagnosis of pancreatitis, lupus, a severe unending Meniere's disease, ringing tinnitus, and Hashimoto's thyroiditis.

Oddly enough, each imbalance in the body has just given more strength to my heart. When love arrives, we build the capacity to listen to ourselves with a merciful ear, to turn to ourselves as we would to our only child, and commit ourselves wholeheartedly to use all we have to support our healing.

On occasion, I was approached in workshops by new agers lathered in their superstitious belief that I must have done some really bad stuff in my past life to have come into this life with so many illnesses. It had to be due to bad karma, they insisted, implying it is all my fault and up to me to reverse.

Stephen said that it may actually be a given part of my "healer's training," taken on as a service to other sentient beings to bring a healing mercy to those who find themselves in similar circumstances.

One can't possibly know the inherited genetic origin of illness. And to those who insist the cause had to be stress, I can only reply that there are too many obscure possible causes to be adamant about unknown origins. It is more appropriate, living in the present, to watch and deepen how the quieting of stress can certainly diminish the effects of disease whatever the hidden cause.

The other end of people's bewilderment about my various seeming frailties is their "How come you always seem so well, so loving and optimistic toward others?" To them, I say that our minds are usually so full that we forget to listen to the whisper of intuition above the din of our fear and feelings of helplessness.

By not rushing into just any treatment offered before researching it and asking pertinent questions, we can exercise our option to remember our greater nature, our original vastness. You can sit quietly and listen to the wisdom of the pain itself, which will reveal the fluctuations of your mental and physical discomfort. You can experience directly how softening eases us, and how resistance amplifies the difficulty, which often turns pain into suffering.

The love that reaches out to pain breaks through. The gift in the wound sends mercy to others. As the process gradually reverses itself, we can *experience* the vastness encouraging us to open the fist cramped around the frightened heart, and to cultivate loving kindness for all the weary beings in the world, ourselves included.

Recent studies confirm what our patients displayed for years: that very few beings really give themselves the love and forgiveness they occasionally offer others. The more one is forgiving and generous to others (and even oneself), the more deeply manifest is the increased capability to heal and the growing capacity for happiness and love.

A Recipe for Self Forgiveness

For the first six months, three times a day, send a few minutes of forgiveness and loving kindness to yourself. Each succeeding six-month period, expand the circle of loving kindness to include your loved ones and those who support your healing. As the heart surrenders its pain, it will begin to send love and acceptance, effortlessly, to yourself and others for the rest of your life.

To touch with mercy that which we have withdrawn from in fear is strong medicine. Instead of letting our pain turn into suffering, we can deal with it directly, as much as possible—maintaining mercy for ourselves and others, during the hard times—softening around unpleasant sensations, one-by-one, as they arise. We note that fear has a tendency to project negative outcomes, so it's important to stay in the moment-to-moment process in which a merciful softness receives sensations into the possibilities of healing. We begin to see our travail not as a phenomenon which separates us from our life, but as a signal to save our life.

Each illness for me was an apprenticeship. Each illness tenderized my heart a bit. Each time my body wisdom called my attention to the work to be done through pain or some threat to its longevity, I received a further initiation into compassion. Feeling mercy spread from one's illness to another, it was no longer just "my pain," with all the trappings of resistance, self-pity, and loss of control, but a sense of "the pain," the Impersonal Universal, inhabiting the lives of so many for whom I felt an empathetic connection.

Each time I had another diagnosis, or even prognosis, there was what I am slightly embarrassed to call a "shamanic apprenticeship." The illness began to remove a brick or two from the Great Wall of isolation behind which I lived in silent anger and merciless self-rejection. At first one feels sorry for themselves, but as I said, eventually that state of mind develops into concern for others too, those experiencing difficult moments in their own lives, as gratitude is found for the little things that were always present but somehow not fully appreciated.

Over the years my feelings of worthlessness were being attacked by sporadic illnesses, which insisted I love myself or die. Many of my most healing insights were preceded by moments of disappointment, and feelings of being lost, before "the cloud of unknowing" parted and let the truth through.

Illness was a teaching in self-awareness. And like any good spiritual teacher it wouldn't let me lie to myself, invoke magical thinking, or blame another for my predicament. I was refused the comfort of secondary benefits like, "Oh, poor Ondrea!" or any projection of another's fear and perhaps even spiritual ignorance in the form of "You've got bad karma or why else would you get so many diagnoses?" In fact, I came to feel my karma was pretty good because these illnesses rarely stuck around for long and I learned so much from them.

Time after time, some other part of my body called on me to become whole, and my immune system hung in there with its weakened arms around me, reminding me to have mercy on myself.

I was a slow learner but an appreciative one. Not that I welcomed illness or was glad to feel sickly at times; indeed it occasionally brought to mind our old friend Rick Field's book when he became seriously ill, *Fuck You Cancer & Other Poems*.

To Tell or Not to Tell

In the oncologists' waiting room again, the pro-active actor, the kind of patient most physicians find irritating, waiting to find out my prognosis from overworked, grief-suppressing doctors.

It was another pivotal moment that would send me home to do more research on the Internet, to consult with knowledgeable friends, and speak with other wayfarers working through leukemia. Another map of the terrain in the lab results—was I going up one side or down the other? It's always a matter of telltale numbers that ascend or descend as is their wont.

As the preliminary cancer counts rose, my thoughts were filled with the potential pain and emotional outpouring that might accompany telling our children and, even more so, our grandchildren, that I have leukemia. Do I tell them or not? In addition to the bewilderment about how my loved ones might take this news was the creeping anxiety that accompanies the prospect of long treatments and extended financial hardship.

I watch my gut tighten like a drum. This was, at this moment anyhow, more intense than even the fear of dying. Something deep inside me feared my loved ones retreating from me more than the reoccurrence of cancer.

We had seen in our years of counseling terminally ill patients that many were surprised by the reaction of family, friends, and coworkers. Some had been embraced, others rejected. Some were brought closer to the heart and accepted as they had never been before, while others had had friends and family turn their backs on them.

I remember how difficult it was to accept the diagnosis of cancer more than thirty years ago, and how deeply it affected my family and friends who stiffened to my predicament. I had made their lives more difficult because I had not accepted the illness myself, so I couldn't communicate what I needed—sometimes the warmth of a hug, at other moments complete seclusion in my original silence—to the frustration of all involved.

The first time around my focus was mostly on a "cure" but now, in what seemed like an incarnation later, I followed the path of healing. This time I expanded my capacity to heal by pulling back on my anger and fear. This time, during morning and evening meditations, I sent love and mercy directly into the center of any sensation I felt to be somehow connected to my cancer, and continued projecting feelings of loving kindness out into the universe, into the hearts of all who might benefit from it.

> *May all beings be free from suffering; May all beings be at peace.*
> *May all beings enter with mercy the pain of the world:*
> *your pain and mine as well.*
> *May all sentient beings be free from suffering,*
> *know the grace of their true nature,*
> *and serve each other in that manner.*

This time I had Stephen and a quickening of the heart from our years of mindfulness meditation and deep consciousness practices that had gradually taught me to trust my process and showed me how to love, even myself, beyond expectation, beyond illness. I sent mercy and kindness into that which I most often sent mercilessness, anger, and tension. I softened around the pain and fear, and explored the different ways I closed off or opened to the healing.

For some, illness is an opportunity to show their love. For others, it becomes the focal point of long submerged fears of death. For some loved ones, it is the opportunity of a lifetime to open their heart in hell; to be present, to allow forgiveness, and to at last become whole. There are those embraced by loved ones with a feeling of never having been heard so deeply before. Many take the opportunity to spend time together and perhaps finish some bit of unfinished business, some unattended grief. Others, regrettably, raise the wall even higher, increasing their absence from the life of the dying person and the rich and often difficult opportunities for growth their presence provides.

When I told my parents, they immediately changed their will. They were worried that if they left me some money it might get "wasted on a lot of useless medical treatments."

THIRTEEN

A Year to Live

STEPHEN AND I HAD been with hundreds of people through the last years of their lives. We wrote *A Year to Live* (published in 1997) as an experiment in the consciousness of living a year as though it was our last, encouraging readers to focus on the impermanence of life, kindly attending to the loose ends of regret, remorse, and missed opportunities.

Though dying can be an unpleasant process, it can be surprisingly satisfactory when met with a merciful awareness, and one better to be encountered now with mercy and forgiveness than on our deathbed when our concentration may be low and self-judgment confusingly high.

As I've said, our patients approaching death often voiced disappointment with their lives—remorse they hadn't done better, been happier, gotten divorced, gotten married, changed jobs, decreased or increased the energy they put into their favorite things, but most of all regret that they hadn't played more and loved more wisely.

Dying can be a time to send love to absent loved ones and to open up to the finishing of unfinished business, which is the fundamental energy that propels forgiveness, and with it, the clear recognition of priorities.

Some people, when they first heard of the book, feared that the practice might draw death close, but for most it drew them even closer to life. One fellow said it allowed him to feel his heartbeat without it beginning to race, that he was less numb to his body and the life force he was so grateful for.

After the book's publication we heard from groups around the country who had committed themselves to share with each other the book's insights and the process of their living a year as if it was their last. People who were young and healthy, as well as those older and less well, equally realized from the practice that there was not a moment to lose to forgive others and reduce the distance between loved ones, to consider if their work was how they wished for their life to unfold, and whether time was bringing them closer to what they loved or driving them further away. As John Lennon said, "Life is what happens to you while you're busy making other plans."

In the course of the year to live practice, in the recognition of priorities, many found out how their desires had formed and/or malformed their lives. They began to address their hidden pain directly and to see how much more there was to learn about how their relationships with others (but primarily themselves) had helped to cause their dissatisfaction. How their desire systems mapped their lives. How the presence or absence of dissatisfaction was most of what they could recall.

Where does all this pain come from? How much of it is not just the inevitable pain of desire, of clinging and condemning, but the inborn pain which entered with us? The pain that is inherent in incarnation. As a technologically oriented friend of mine put it, "We come preloaded with our prehistory!"

The origins of most mental discomforts are traceable to the dynamic network of wanting, having, and losing an object of desire— having what we have longed for; feeling a stressful need to protect it; finding it broken, lost, unreachable; or never having had it in the first place. Or conversely, but just as painfully, getting something we don't want or something we even hoped to elude. Pain gone unexplored or long resisted becomes suffering.

Still, different wisdom teachers tell us there is another kind of pain, an unnamed pain they call "suffering, suffering," whose origin goes so deep that it apparently precedes birth and seems to be inherent in being born. This delayed stress syndrome of our birth can extend all the way from our inborn fear and unwillingness to be born to our terror of not being at all. A fear greater than death, as many believe, that exists even after the falling away of the body, as a continual unfolding of consciousness.

This "suffering, suffering" the teachers talk about, wagging their metaphorical finger, is nothing personal; it just comes with the territory, reinforcing other forms of suffering as well as providing us with questions that propel a lifetime of valuable inquiry.

Desire naturally breeds attachment: wanting this, not wanting that. Attachment/desire is not good or bad; it's just painful. One can experience the process of leaning toward what one wishes and pulling back from what one hopes will not occur by observing the belly softening and hardening with the state of satisfaction and dissatisfaction. Our day a roller coaster of getting and not having. It makes us seasick. Liking and disliking all day long leaving us, not at all surprisingly exhausted.

> *You want what you don't have, and you don't have what you want, and so you suffer and continue to suffer. It is so perplexing, why not simply reverse it? Why not "want" what you have and "not want" what you don't have? You could be happy. Freedom is here for the taking. You want little things when you could have the entire universe—eternity, eternal life—take that.*
> —Nisargadatta Maharaj

One of the problems and dissatisfactions wanting brings is our addiction to the state of mind we call "satisfaction." We know so little about our inner workings that when a powerful engine drives an action toward fulfillment, it's called satisfaction, and it is almost completely obscured by the urgency that accompanies this addiction.

If I was ever going to find peace, I needed to understand the mechanics of wanting. To recognize that oddly enough, the very nature of wanting was a feeling of not having, a feeling of dissatisfaction, until satisfaction is at hand.

Wanting something, anything, maybe a new car, we want it, we want it, we want it (a very unsatisfactory state). Then, as the object of desire approaches, our internal engine racing, "We almost have it." At that point of expectation our pulse, heartbeat, indeed our whole system, is on a magnified alert. Then here it is at last so shiny and wonderful! Finally it arrives with our name on the owner's certificate. Desire is absent. Satisfaction!!!

Closely observed, one notices that satisfaction, pleasure, entails the momentary absence of the pain of not having what we want. It deeply relieves the pressure of our wanting. This feeling of delight, this sigh of relief, is actually the joy of no longer blocking the light beyond.

Satisfaction is a glimpse of our underlying nature, the experience of which is unending gratification. It has been said, "When desire is stilled, held quietly in the heart, the whole world awakens and the unseen brushes our cheek." In the bliss that we call "divine" by so many names, we experience the momentary joy of our true, unencumbered nature.

Ahhh, the satisfaction of that shiny new car parked out there in front of the house. Ahhh, satisfaction, the gut releasing the tension of wanting, just enjoying the soft belly of having. Until the inhabitation of ownership guarding against an attack against loss becomes itself an object of dissatisfaction. And what is that?! What is that dog doing raising his leg on our brand new car? Is he pissing on our satisfaction in a most unsatisfactory way? We want him to empty his bladder elsewhere, we want to park the car around the corner; we want to restore the shine! A moment of satisfaction followed by an hour of dissatisfaction. It could be our new dream job, dream girl, boyfriend, insight or enlightenment, or anything we cling to, that impermanence pulled beyond our grasp, leaving rope burns that create scars across our lifeline.

One of the most skillful lessons of *A Year to Live* practice is that the secret of life is "Pay attention." And to give ourselves permission to live our life like a love song.

Forgiveness

In my youth, when I was first overcome by sorrow, I did not know where forgiveness resided, so I looked outside for it. I asked God for forgiveness for my so-called "sins." But I got a busy signal! I think everyone must have been trying to get through that day. I wasn't sure what my sins were, but I felt I must have quite a few of them, feeling as bad as I did. I prayed every morning and every night for forgiveness of my unknown malady. Kafkaesque.

When I met Stephen, I told him I would sometimes get so down on myself I asked Jesus for forgiveness, but it didn't seem to help. He suggested that, instead of praying to Jesus, I pray with Jesus. He was practicing a Buddhist forgiveness meditation and found it quite useful. He said that when Jesus said, "Judge not, lest you be judged," he was imparting a great truth. The judging mind doesn't know the difference between you and the person sitting next to you. To the judging mind, everyone is the other.

Stephen said don't try to force forgiveness at the beginning, that forgiveness is too important to make it a contest with God or yourself. He said, easy does it. Work with it as you would lift weights in a gym; don't try to lift the thousand pounder at the beginning. Don't go for the inhumanity of man right off the bat. Try the five-pound weight, the small stuff, like your shoes are too tight or that the bus driver was harsh when he told you to move to the back of the bus this morning. If you start too big, you will end up herniating yourself and never work out again. You will lose faith. So start small, meeting the burgeoning sound and fury around you with a little softness, a bit of morning mercy. Allow yourself a dollop of forgiveness for the tightness of a noisy world. And let it build slowly. The heart is a very practical muscle. It grows from responding to difficulty with kindness; it freezes from the mindless reaction to pain that causes more of the same. Forgiveness is the active verb of the noun mercy.

Working with the five- and ten-pound insults, the lesser indifferences, will build our tolerance for a world on fire with ignorance and violence. Slowly, you can turn toward the needs of others and yourself, bind the wounds that cripple us all, and meet with loving kindness and forgiveness the fears that drive everybody toward the edge. It's not like we will always be able to change course at our whim, but we may be able to steer clear sooner, or find a bridge to cross. As one of our teachers said, "The mind creates the abyss, the heart crosses it."

I started small with forgiveness, beginning with rude acquaintances, working through letting go, letting be, and forgiving self-serving friends before dealing with the rancor of dishonesty and greed so confused in our culture, until my heart was strong enough for the dynamism of family issues. Another in the group asked how long it took for me to break through. I answered, much to their disappointment, that I was still working on it. And I asked their forgiveness for not giving them more confidence in a quicker fix, but such issues for some are not a bump in the road, but a crossing of a grand chasm.

It can take years before we can get our hands around the deepest injuries we have tried so diligently to bury out of sight, beneath the hardpan of the injured mind, just hoping for another day's survival. But for most, the work we do on ourselves can allow us, at times, to give others a hand. When they are lost and can't find their own map, asking for directions can be a momentous act of bravery and strength.

Someone in one of our retreats said that the forgiveness practice allowed him to forgive the God that didn't forgive him. This unfinished business with God was an issue that arose many times. It reminded us of a long-broken-down temple in India that we were told had been abandoned and was never rebuilt "because of a fight with the gods."

We often run our relationships as if they were a business. I'll give you four if you give me four, but if it seems you only gave me three, you owe me. An unforgiven debt arises in the Karma Savings & Loan. "You owe me" is resentment. "I owe you" is guilt. And the longer our interactions go on like this, the more impoverished we become. We lose our balance, the heart is thrown askew. The gut tightens. The eyes cannot open fully. But forgiveness rebalances the mind and brings kindness to the senses.

Forgiveness decomposes the armoring over the heart. It allows an unimagined kindness to seep into the lowest sense of self. Judging ourselves, we judge others. Self-forgiveness is not self-indulgent but is a service to the world, a means of opening our life and a benefit to others.

Oddly enough, the true magic begins when, quite to our amazement, we discover that it is our attachment to our suffering, *our own negative attachment,* that holds our suffering in place.

The automatic pushing away of the unwanted displays this negative attachment. Our resistance is our attachment. It reveals our natural aversion to pain and the "knee jerk reaction" it engenders—we are angry at our anger, fearful of our fear, anxious about our anxiety, judging judgment, we relate *from* rather than *to* our confusing predicament. As we perpetually lunge at our unfinished business, we are like someone who, having been stung, walks up and punches the hive. Mercy for ourselves, mercy sent into our open wounds, mercy for us all, a thousand times stung.

Stephen wrote that when an early teacher first said to him, "Be kind to yourself," his knees began to buckle and he had to sit down. It had never occurred to him before.

We may think forgiveness isn't necessary, that it might be a sign of weakness, but even the best of relationships between family, friends, and lovers, because of subtly differing desire systems, may well have some slight unfinished business that needs tending. This gentle, daily forgiveness, as an experiment in conscious compassion, can keep our life current.

As we gradually begin the forgiveness practice, we notice we are not forgiving the action, but the actor. We are not condoning cruelty; we're forgiving someone for being cruel (even ourselves) as the revered Buddhist monk Thich Nhat Hanh points out, "those whose heart could not yet see."

We can forgive someone who stole from us without excusing stealing per se. By practicing forgiveness, we are not reinforcing oppressive or injurious action. We may, after considerable processing of emotion, forgive someone whose heart was so obstructed, so unable to see beyond its sorrow, that they caused injury to another. We are forgiving the person, not the action. The irony is that I might be able to forgive someone who kills without approving of killing in any way.

It can be unskillful to go directly to the forgiveness practice before addressing the afflictive states which block and limit entrance into the open-minded heart. This is the work of cultivating a merciful awareness capable of investigating the pains and traumas hidden in our marrow and deep tissues. Discovering in the muscle shield of the abdomen that the long-recommended softening of the belly practice helps release the holding and resistance, in a manner that softens the past as well.

We learn to forgive the past and all the ghosts, living and dead, who have not had the benefit of mercy. And we let the ghost of ourselves be forgiven as well. We allow ourselves to imagine being touched by their love and their wish for our well-being.

We must test everything in our heart to see for ourselves what a month of silent, daily forgiveness might do to the flow of our life. See for ourselves what soft belly reoccurring throughout the day does to that day. How much more love than loss might be found. When we use soft belly as a reference point, we don't suppress our feelings; we give them room to breathe.

A Day of Forgiveness

What would it be like if we had a day of mindful forgiveness? A day without anger or remorse? A day in which we meet the moment with respect, honoring all those who cross our path? To peer through the shadows reality casts and see the original heart behind it all? To see how we cannot see. To discover how to love by watching how unloving we can be. A day of making amends to others by touching those around us with the forgiveness we wish for ourselves. And amends to the earth from which we take so much and return so little. Asking and offering forgiveness in this world, which my teacher calls "the ghost plane," so little of our true selves showing.

A day of treating others as we wish to be treated. Remembering that they too, no matter how difficult at times it may be to perceive, lament not waking up to a day in a life of love. A day when the still, small voice within remembers that to forgive others opens the door to self-forgiveness.

Part of my birth into a life of love is to allow myself out of hiding.

It would be ideal if I could just let go of afflictive states, but the considerable momentum of negative identification with these feelings is not so easily dissuaded. Sometimes, before, when I could simply be mindful of them, I could enter these states with a liberating awareness. But I had to learn to clear the way by skillful means. I learned to meet merciless judgment of myself and others with mercy. Just as softening the belly initiates a letting go in the mind and body, which can be felt in the heart, its equivalent in the work of forgiveness softens the holding in the mind, which can be felt in the letting go of the hardness in my belly.

The practice is not to submerge anger or guilt, but to bring it to the surface, so it is accessible to healing. Not that these qualities will disappear, but that we will no longer be surprised by them, or unable to meet them with mercy, even with a sense of humor, for the mind seems to have a mind of its own.

If, at first, forgiveness seems a little awkward, even self-serving when turned toward oneself, that is simply an indication of how little we have considered the possibility and how foreign loving kindness has become.

On a day of mindful forgiveness, instead of being seduced into mind-chatter that tries to convince me that the "I am" of anger is noble, I would recognize that each state of mind has its own unique body pattern and be able to approach each emotion as its imprint in the body. Allowing awareness to survey each outline and clear the approach to the heart, loosening identification with the states so that anger and self-pity might pass through the mind without becoming angry or pitiful.

Just as clarity brings with it a loving sense of openness in the body and mind, anger and fear, in their turn, close the mind, tighten the jaw and belly, and leave little room for anything else. Becoming aware of these roadblocks to the heart, these hindrances to happiness, opens the path forward.

During the course of a mindful forgiveness day, I reflected on what the word "forgiveness" might mean as various people come to mind, some invited, some lurking just offstage, waiting for an opportunity to make their case. As an experiment in happiness when I noticed their presence, I touched them with forgiveness, even the closest friends who I imagined needed no such greeting. Watching to see if even my loved ones might resist being forgiven, I simply said to them, "I forgive you," and watched my mind's response, noting whatever unexpected, unfinished business began its spin. I noted whatever friends, coworkers, family, old flames, or old flame extinguishers came to mind. And when we do it, don't be surprised that you are surprised at what occurs in the shadows when you say "I forgive you." To you or anyone else.

Forgiveness Finishes Unfinished Business

Forgiveness changes the world; it lets us see where we stand. When I began focusing forgiveness on my mother, reaching out to her from that state of mind, I said, "Mom, I forgive you for any way you ever caused me pain, intentionally or unintentionally, through whatever you said or did." Saying it slowly, bringing her image to mind, I held the intention to let go of whatever kept her out of my heart. The release and opening of the anger and fear gradually became more genuine, dropping through levels and levels of release, the breath became smoother, and then in my open-mindedness I heard her say, "You forgive me? How dare you!" and my belly turned to stone. And then I remembered how long these barriers have been up and how long it might take to tear down the wall. We never know where our next teaching might unexpectedly come from.

When the belly softens the tension and begins to melt, the armor clatters to the floor, the breath reaching down into the body, picking up bits of grace as it passes. It gives birth to me from a deepening new breath, a natural breath that does not attempt to shape or control the breath but just lets it breathe itself. A long unattended sorrow finds mercy from one end of the star-born body to the other. The difference from one incarnation to another is just a breath away.

The more often we lose our way, then find our way back again, the wider the passage becomes. And then, instead of constricting the buttocks and the gut each time that the heart becomes obscured by doubt or fear, anger or judgment, we set ourselves free with "Ah yes, anger, envy, fear again. Big Surprise!" which of course is no surprise at all—a wry acceptance of the passing show, noting with each changing state, pleasant or unpleasant, the familiarity of the same old painful states with the recognition, "Big Surprise!" And life becomes a moment-to-moment surprise, instead of an ongoing indignation.

"Yes, Ma, you, I forgive you, and wish you to find it in your heart to forgive me for whatever prompted that awful resentment, whatever made you sweat beneath your armor. I didn't suppose we would ever meet where love might slip past our defenses and quite unexpectedly touch each other. But let the fist open, exposing a hidden empathy."

During this forgiveness practice we recognize how our lack of forgiveness, our indifference, our impatience with each other's hearts, causes considerable suffering in the world.

And we begin to become the person we always wanted to be.

The *Sutras* say there are skillful ways of looking at illness. One way to relate to illness is that it burns off the karmic life momentum accrued from previous events. By softening to accept the push and pull that comes with confronting illness, meeting with mercy the minor, sometimes major, compulsive disgust which discomfort provides, we begin to see ourselves grasping instead of letting go, being jealous instead of generous, negative instead of accepting, judgmental instead of open-minded, or cold-hearted instead of merciful.

Illness has the potential to clear karma. But if karma were the only origin of illness, considering all the times we have tripped over our forgetfulness and selfishness, all the times we have been unable to see in the shadows of our fear and profound unkindness to ourselves, we surely would have died at birth.

Karma has a math of its own that even Einstein and others of great wisdom admit they cannot tabulate. Some of the vilest people may have astonishingly good health.

Illness gets our attention, and where there is an increase in focus, there is an opportunity for clarity, and where clarity grows, perhaps wisdom grows with it. An opportunity arises to send kindness into all those places the mind derides when ill, all the places the mind has unskillfully retreated from, an opportunity to enter the abandoned parts of ourselves with loving kindness, to soothe the pain that tends to close the heart, mind, and body.

Some who are ill feel betrayed by the body but learn to observe how the body swoons when softened and forgiven. Though it may seem counterintuitive, it makes *perfect* sense to open the heart to pain and illness, to direct mercy into those areas which have panicked, tripped, and fallen over themselves trying to escape.

Every part of us is doing the best it can under the circumstances. Sometimes bringing our attention to where it hurts, one part of us will collaborate with another, carrying the softness cultivated in the belly, say, to soothe isolated discomforts elsewhere.

The body is healed by the mind, the mind by the heart, and the heart by the unadulterated vastness of being.

Ideas of enlightenment may entangle the mind in an anticipation of some dreamed-of result instead of an investigation of the present reality. Forgive the ignorance around the concept of enlightenment. Forgiveness of illness, unfinished melodramas, and our willingness to do more damage to ourselves calls us to our healing and directs us toward something often less painful than the past.

The Practical and Etheric Advantages of Forgiveness . . . A Daily Kindness

Practice self-forgiveness every morning, before you get out of bed, and every evening before sleep.

Each night I ask God, Buddha, Mary, and my spiritual advisors, ancestors, and role models to help me cultivate forgiveness and loving kindness for myself.

Turn to yourself, and using your own first name say I forgive you to you:
"May I be at peace, may I be forgiven for all those moments when my heart
could not yet see. May I be free from suffering, may I be forgiven for what-
ever I may have done intentionally or unintentionally that caused another
pain. May I know mercy for myself and all sentient beings."

Everyone forgives at their own pace. Entering the stream of mercy and loving kindness, of forgiveness and letting go, we eventually confront the most difficult character of all: ourselves.

If we can forgive ourselves, we can forgive anyone.

In my early years of this practice I felt no profound forgiveness, but with practice it did change. Guilt, even shame, began to matriculate to the state of remorse, a much softer form of judgment. A great relief to our, often, miserable self-image.

If we did no practice other than forgiveness and loving kindness, we might well free ourselves from that infolded unkindness by which we may unfortunately identify ourselves. When we learn how to allow a moment of anger to pass through the mind without becoming angry, a twisting moment of fear to pass through without becoming afraid, further along the spectrum we will be able to allow a moment of love to stay just a moment longer.

Complete self-forgiveness is easier to intellectually understand than to actualize. If possible, it means that we forgive ourselves and all others on every level for all we all have ever done or said. To learn to forgive ourselves at these deepest levels helps release our deepest guilt, and one does this practice "until the body drops." Some add, "Even perhaps a little longer."

The Dalai Lama says one of his greatest regrets is the impossibility of retrieving untoward comments. Everyone loses their balance at one time or another. That's why it is easier to forgive others for their missteps in the dance than our clumsy selves. Letting go of self-recrimination and offering a poultice of mercy draw out the residual toxins of a life of self-rejection and repeatedly put ourselves out of our heart. We can never do too much forgiveness for "I and other."

We go from the one-size-fits-all constrictions of the small mind to the generous expanse, the open-heartedness, of the big mind. It's all based on our intentions.

While some people might find it discouraging to imagine any practice taking years, even lifetimes, to integrate, to sink from the mind into the heart, indeed, in some cosmologies a single lifetime on one plane may be equivalent to a quick breakfast on another.

FOURTEEN

Healing Is Our Birthright

HALF TRUTHS ARE THE most dangerous; by accepting a half truth, one may be swallowed whole. The belief that they "created their own reality" has left many wracked with guilt and helplessness, unable to go beyond blaming the victim, themselves. Recognizing and acknowledging that decreasing stress can aid in healing, some jump to the unfortunate conclusion that therefore stress causes all illness.

The whole truth is that we don't *create* our illness, we *affect* it. We have the inherent power to soften around pain, and even cancer, with a remarkable mercy that physician friends have shown can open the blood flow, thus accessing the immune system, where it is most needed.

When spurred on by my "knowing" that there had to be more to healing than the doctor's frightening small-mindedness, I came across Stephen Jay Gould's experience and insights. The renowned philosopher and anthropologist spoke about the power of confidence in one's self to overcome the confusion that doctors sometimes impart to their patients. After being assured he only had a few months to live from an "intractable cancer," Gould lived twenty more years. "Those two decades, from a patient's point of view," he said, "had more healing in it than most would have been able to recognize. Optimism holds great potential."

Gould found that optimism reinforces the best of what is to be found in our conditioning and diminishes that which tries to defend illness. He was not talking about blind faith, but trust in finding a way through the labyrinth of forgetfulness, to the center of our original power to take the heart past the pessimistic mind that holds onto the idea that we somehow deserve to suffer. Pessimism is a dark comrade of illness and a life-degrading lack of self-regard.

Sometimes, we have to lead ourselves past our mercilessness, to find our remarkable, innate healing power. Like Plato's shadow lost in the cave before it remembers to turn toward the light, the power to send love into the wild multiplicity of cancer or even the self-hatred that obscures the healing we took birth for.

Taking to heart Gould's comment that "the median isn't the message," it has been called "the wisest, most humane thing ever written about cancer and statistics." Gould said statistical averages are just misleading abstractions that don't encompass the full range of variations of an individual's process. Mark Twain said, "There are lies, damned lies, and statistics!"

It is now years since the half-knowing doctor shook me up, and I am still feeling and looking very well, most of the time. Even today, my energy is still pretty smooth. The doctors marvel that I have had this leukemia for twelve years and have done so well, without any debilitating side effects from the sixteen monoclonal antibody infusions. Though we keep an eye on the slow increase in blood test indicators for cancer, none of the treatments they said might eventually be necessary have so far been called for. The cancer is in the body, not in my heart.

My doctors told me I must have great genes to fight off so many illnesses. This makes me thank my parents for, besides half-a-lifetime of heart-wearying resentment, also the genes to fight off illness. I think a cup of forgiveness all around is called for.

Stephen has undergone many of these discomforts and illnesses with me, all these years. And now, the cancer I thought I would never have to work through again has reappeared. Because I had health issues on and off much of my life, Stephen joined me in my healer's training. He entered with me the various phases of my unpleasant body experiences. I think he was going through a sort of survival and surrender training himself.

There is an ancient idea that over each of our shoulders there forms two long lines behind us, one of our mother's ancestors, the other of our father's, both lines offering prayers that we will be the ones to break the family dysfunction.

Although a lot of concepts and terms are being floated about, perhaps the following techniques applied with a willingness to heal and a respect for our pain may hold some of the keys we're looking for.

There is an experience, a sleep paralysis, in which one's mind can awaken while the body is still asleep. This can be an opportunity to practice dying while staying alive, watching the mind/body from a clear awareness. In this state, no matter how hard you try, you cannot move or wake up. It can be quite disconcerting, at first, but when you develop mindfulness of the link between intentional causation and movement, it can actually be fascinating.

I've had this experience on several occasions. At first I was fearful and struggled with great effort to move my body or speak. After repeatedly being frustrated by the helplessness of "brain over matter," I realized it was a rare opportunity to apply my meditative practice and surrender, even practice dying, as many teachers have recommended. As I lay there, I was no longer my body. My mind released resistance and sank into my heart. Odd as it may seem, I did not even want the condition to disappear.

And just as I often watched my mind like one would watch a freight train passing at a railroad crossing, I watched my thoughts as if they were boxcars trundling by, noticing what was written on them, but also maintaining focus straight ahead as they disappeared down the line. Noting the content of the boxcars as I would thoughts, but more interested in the flow, I discovered the marvelous open spaces between the freight-laden cars, like the clarity between thoughts. A glimpse of the vastness beyond observing for a moment, what laid on the other side of "the train of thought." Seeing beyond thinking, I saw the light flickering between passing "thoughts."

A predominant healer's training over the past years has been directed at how well one can be in the heart and mind, even when the body is pulsing in pain. Over the years, the doctors have marveled at my quick recoveries. I almost always looked healthy and had more energy than the healthy people around me. I believe it was because of Stephen's and my love and my meditation on the body sensations while sending forgiveness and prayer into the difficulty that kept me in balance.

This apparently didn't stop other diseases from showing up, but it certainly changed their intensity and duration. It gave me a method to deal with the madness of impermanence.

Compassionate Intent

Recently, continuing my investigation into the dreary prognosis given at the first hospital I went to, I was on the last leg of a train trip to the highly recommended Mayo Clinic in Rochester, Minnesota, for additional measurement of the extent of the leukemia. The outcome turned out to be considerably more positive than the earlier prognosis.

I have a kind of leukemia, like many do, that apparently cannot be cured, but may, even with questionable "markers," be repeatedly treatable.

Sitting in a coach seat among a wide variety of travelers, I made small talk with a lovely woman sitting beside me who asked where I was going. When I said, without adding my purpose, that I was headed toward Rochester, Minnesota, she said spontaneously, "Ah, you're going to the Mayo Clinic!"

Nodding in a knowing fashion, which demonstrated an implicit recognition that I must have some serious illness, she asked if she could pray for me and sent a palpable love into my held hand. She called others to join us. The passenger car filled with silence. A glorious prayer for my well-being sped down the tracks.

And just like the little blessings of those we met when first going into the cancer center in Santa Fe, the prayer generated by these lovely hearts warmed me to the divine in every moment.

This was not the only bit of grace along the way. In the lobby of the oncology wing of the Mayo Clinic, a couple next to me asked with no further ado if they could pray with me. When they got down on their knees, I followed and there we were joined by many others in a prayer of well-being and gratitude. It turned out to be an unforeseeably beautiful trip.

Even after four days of testing, when I arrived home, I could still feel their blessings and compassionate intent, could still feel their hugs like way stations on my somewhat anxious trip toward the unknown. At the kind oasis of the very caring Mayo Clinic, their prayers may have been answered, as my situation turned from a fatal prognosis to more of an infection-wary well-tended chronic leukemia.

Because I have done so unexpectedly well in the course of slowing down the progress of the leukemia, it is impossible to attribute this grace to any single cause. So many highly qualified healers and clinics have attended to my needs, I can only bow to them all with gratitude. From skilled, compassionate physicians, highly regarded Native American shaman, a long-distance Hispanic wizard, two psychic energy transmitters (one of whom related that he had erased black lines from my aura), a Buddhist nun who had done wonders for friends, and a New York Jew in a jungle shaman's lineage flanked by two wolves, all of whom I have considered recommending to others.

An old friend, Chris, who knew of my illness, emailed me that he had gotten us admission to see John of God, the highly regarded Brazilian healer. He knew I would make every excuse not to go, so he had preemptively made a checklist and read it off to me as I laughed and had to relent. I said yes and off we went.

John of God channels a few long-deceased doctors who come through him to manifest the well-documented healings of many who are quite seriously ill. Even staunch disbelievers who have visited with him have come back convinced that he had something very substantial to offer. The group of a thousand we were part of emanated a remarkably loving essence. I prayed for three days and nights to Mary, for my own healing and the healing of all that were present. I felt a great deal of love from the group and especially for my dear friend who gave me this gift.

Healing may come from the most unexpected of directions. One healer I was brought to, a very kind fellow, had ten people in a hut overnight while he chanted, sang, and prayed. It felt just right and I was quite enthusiastic. He was insightful and loving, as was the rest of the group in the hut.

The morning after this experience Chris and I walked down the beach to get breakfast. I was anxious, and when I feel like that, I often spin out a bit and repeat myself. I told my friend, the kindest of people, that I was sorry. He, as full of healing as any of the shaman I had met, said it wasn't a problem for him, that my repetition was just fine, as it gave him "further chances to hear me and better find answers to my questions." In his acceptance of me, at a time when I felt so little of that for myself, waves of healing passed through my body. It was the perfect "as is" response that so defines love.

I have been blessed to have many beings known and unknown praying for me. Because of their extraordinary compassion, my body opens further and further to unexpected healings from whatever direction they arrive.

This book is not the tale of "me" overcoming hardship, or the "slings and arrows of outrageous fortune." This is a love story.

Last Visit

Because my mother had been so mean-spirited to me all her life, I put up a protective wall over which I attempted to launch an occasional compliment now and again, a thoughtful birthday or anniversary present, but to no avail. I tried less and less as I grew older, and after many years I stopped altogether, for which I sometimes felt remorse. In later years, to calm her agitation, I attempted to apologize for being who I was, knowing all the time that I was the person I was always meant to be.

My mother was not open to forgiveness, either for her or from her. After I apologized a few times, just to cover all the bases, I asked for her forgiveness, but she never replied, not with a nod or any sort of response. She was deaf to any words from my heart; she just walked away.

I must repeat here that one needs to be mindful in forgiving the abuser so as not to slip into the tar pool of self-condemnation or self-recrimination as though one had been complicit with the act. Let the abuser carry their own luggage.

When I last visited my mother, she was actually trying to be friendlier. We spoke for about ten minutes about what we might do the next day, and then she abruptly said, "That's enough, go to bed!" It was all she could muster. For a moment there was a glimmer of light, like a flashlight whose batteries have become depleted.

She was always proud of never saying she was sorry about anything to anyone, to which my father in his numbness would nod in agreement.

When my mother was in her late forties, her own mother, who had deserted her at two years old and whom she had put out of her heart long ago, was dying. My mother refused to forgive her or even visit. She said her mother had left her with a chip on her shoulder, which she never got over. It is called lost child syndrome, the abandoned abandoning, and is a keepsake passed like a genetic disorder from parent to child.

I remember one of our patients who spoke of being the only one of her always-hateful mother's children who had agreed to tend her in her final months. Her mother cursed her as she died: "May you be reborn in hell!" Meanwhile the daughter, who had done a great deal of work on forgiveness and cultivating inner strength, mindfulness, and loving kindness, sat quietly next to the mental agony of her mother and sent love into her, praying for her mom's well-being. She said it could have been one of the worst moments of her life, but instead it had been one of the best. When she told her story to the group, everyone took healing from the beauty of her spirit.

In her seventy-fifth year, my mother contracted emphysema. It's odd; when one is facing the prospect of losing one who has been so central, either for the good or the bad, the past often softens and allows mercy to inhabit some closed-off places. Ironically, the physician treating my mother in her final years recommended she begin taking Prozac daily. She said it made her feel better. "I never knew I was depressed!" she said, too late surprised.

A year later, when she became more ill, Stephen and I offered to have my parents come to New Mexico and live with us, but quite understandably, my mother wanted to be in her own home where my father could take complete care of her. And besides, she added, her emphysema required that she live at sea level. (I think perhaps she was trying to be kinder to me.)

For the next five years, my father did all the cleaning and cooking, and she was grateful that he would do so much. Then after a series of strokes, one day she slept and never awoke again. She was in a coma for ten days before she dropped her body.

I intended to fly to California to say good-bye, but the family dictum of "show no emotion" held fast to the end. The excuse I was given for my not coming out was that because she was already in a coma, it would be no use for me to visit. I reminded my father of how long I had worked with people in comas, but he was adamant. He didn't want me at the hospital and, although I pushed to come for even a very short visit, he said no. He wanted no extra emotion. That was his way. Frustrated, I had to honor it. I knew if I pushed any harder, I would just lose connection with him, so I continued to speak to him regularly and knew I could say good-bye to mother from my home.

When I didn't hear from him for five days, I called to see how things were going with my mother. He told me she had died five days before and was already cremated. I was very disappointed that even in death I couldn't break their lifelessness.

Her wish of never becoming "an old woman of eight-three" was fulfilled; she died the day before her birthday.

My father asked me to take care of their ashes when he died, to mix his with hers and have them buried in a military cemetery, to inscribe his army rank, their names, and most importantly, the words, "Eternally Together" on their marker. My parents were an ideal teaching in helplessness and love; I wouldn't have changed it for anything.

Irony after irony, the family life/death style continued to manifest and even expand. Beyond belief, and with stunning surprise, the family maintained their toxic dynamic by telling me repeatedly that my father was still at home and could not come to the phone because he was sleeping. I called them again and again, until at last I was told he had died six days before! I had been excluded once again! I was so fortunate to be at the bedside of so many beautiful beings dying, yet deprived of support and closure with my parents.

Such an unforeseen circumstance as being unable to attend the death of a loved one can often be balanced out with daily loving kindness and forgiveness meditations. The Tibetans suggest forty-nine days of reminding the deceased that they themselves are the bright light first viewed upon dying, the pure luminescence of mercy and compassion, the essence of mind many call the heart. Some choose to encourage them to see themselves as the beloved of the Beloved. Most in the Tibetan Buddhist tradition attempt to remind the dearly departed that in the afterlife, as in life itself, we find the deepest meanings and furthest insights through the depth of awareness brought to mind, that indeed the whole world is "Mind only." We are more than we ever imagined ourselves to be and a good deal closer to the essential core of Being.

When We Meditate

Call the heart forward, entice the spirits, climb slippery mountains,
feel this body flickering sorrow gravity in the bones
feel the breath in the belly or nostrils, choose one
and stay there five years.

Not breath thoughts
but the sensation accompanying the beginning middle and end
of each in-breath each out-breath
and the space between
where thinking wriggles free.
Returning a thousand times breath breathing
itself sensations sensing themselves floating in the vastness.
Even some idea of who this is floating by, thinking itself vanishing in space.
Dissolving in impermanence. Watching consciousness dream world

after world, self after self,
unconvinced.
Recognizing that what we are looking for is
that which is looking stops the breath and reminds the heart.

FIFTEEN

Hermit Lovers in the Spirit World

WHEN ALL OF OUR children left the roost, I put an ad in the local newspaper looking for an isolated piece of well-wooded, heavily out-cropped mountain land on which to homestead. And remarkably we found exactly what we were looking for! We found it—or it found us—three miles down a dirt road that crossed through our Picuris Pueblo neighbor's tribal lands.

Years of emergency phone calls and long unburdening on our Hanuman Foundation Dying Project phone (which we wrote about in *Meetings at the Edge*) left us ready to replace the metallic ringing of the phone with the soft oceanic sound of the wind through canyon pines.

With an old tractor, we smoothed the woodcutters' road, hauled in a twenty-five-year-old trailer, and anchored it beside an eighty-foot high outcropping. We took large portions of the walls off the trailer and replaced them with double pane glass and sliding windows for lots of light and increased solar heating. We double insulated the structure and enclosed it in a post-and-beam wooden house-like structure. It was toasty and solid and relatively inexpensive.

Before we could bring the animals over, we had to contract with a local well driller who banged away for a few days until he hit solid rock, replaced his drill bit, and said he wanted to quit at ninety feet, which offered only a slight trickle of water that could slowly accumulate in a storage tank. That would have meant not much of a garden and not enough water for the animals or regular amenities like washing and cleaning, but the driller told us he was reluctant to go farther.

That night, I had a dream that we would hit big water at 235 feet. We asked the driller to keep going, saying we would recompense him for any further broken drill bits. We hit diamond-clear water at 236. Stephen teased me that I was "way off."

When we first came to the land, we had to learn to live more consciously. We had to ration water and electricity, all of which was soon to be corrected by adding more solar panels. The benefit was an increase in showers, books read more easily at night, and music gratefully received.

We borrowed an animal trailer to transport the llamas and miniature donkeys from our old house thirty-five miles away and built a small barn and a large fenced area for their new home. We gave the parrots and other birds from the aviary to homes where birds would be well tended.

The Llamas

Llamas hum. They stand heads above the dozen miniature donkeys and the hinny Ke Jay (Hosanna!), who is the daughter of the miniature horse, Yeshe. The tallest of the two llamas, Buddy-Buddy, a three-year-old male, liked me a good deal more than he cared for Stephen. Twice he bounced Stephen off fence posts as they played chase through the field, Buddy waiting for Stephen to breathlessly almost catch up before dancing away with the agility of an antelope. Buddy was a sprinter; Stephen would collapse exhausted and laughing till his side hurt in the middle of the meadow as Buddy came back around to challenge him to another run. Although he probably saw him as male competition, Buddy never let Stephen have the worst he could have offered—the particularly foul projectile contents of his ruminant-filled stomach. Buddy would spray a bit of saliva now and again, but never the treacherous goo.

In our previous home just outside Taos, most afternoons at three, the llamas, donkeys, horse, and mule, "the cavalcade" as we called them, would trundle off to the other end of the acres to stand beneath an old cottonwood tree to greet and snuffle the children passing by on their way home from school. It was a giggling delight to the mostly local farm kids who had never seen such a long-necked, big-eyed fuzzy critter. When the llamas were moved to our mountain hermit-age, we were told the children would wait on the road by the fence and call out to them to come say hello.

As members of the camel family, llamas "kush," kneel down on their front legs and let their rump settle in behind them. We could play with the donkeys in chase-and-catch games, even hide-and-go-seek, but once Buddy settled in, no matter how we tugged or cajoled him, he would turn his head and have none of it. My frustration reminded me that one of my teachers used to say, "The mind has a mind of its own." And when I might complain to myself that this was "the stupidest of llamas," I could hear my teacher's thin laugh, adding that "the observed is the observer."

Soon we found that my only real control over Buddy was to completely withdraw my attention from him. He could not stand to be snubbed. If I walked by him without saying hello, sometimes he would start to sprint away, inviting me to chase him. But if I started to sing or read a poem to the other animals gathering in the field, he might approach, humming just offstage.

Once, Stephen was invited to be on a panel with the Dalai Lama, and during a lunch break, His Holiness asked me what sort of work I did. Momentarily losing context, I replied, "We raise llamas." He looked at me over his glasses and lifted an eyebrow like the Sword of Damocles until I realized the misunderstanding and began to laugh. I explained what I meant, and his translator and then he joined in the laughter. This man, who says his only religion is kindness, knows well the tender interconnection between humankind and nature. He knows that becoming still we learn to hear; he knows the effect of love on matter.

One thought dominos into the next, as I recall that Stephen and I met at the retreat center on Lama Mountain. In so many ways llamas and their namesakes have given us much of what we hold precious in this world.

Reconnecting

In our new home, Stephen and I would hear phantom phones ringing when there were none and ghostly motor rumblings though our nearest neighbor was two-and-a-half miles away. It would take awhile for the natural rhythms to gradually awaken and the remnant echo of phones and passing traffic to subside into the in- and out-breath.

How disconnected we had become in our daily routine of counseling, writing, teaching, maintaining the Hanuman Foundation Dying and Grief phoneline 24/7, from the simple quiet. Only when we meditated did we actually feel the quiet, but the rest of the day was spent in unbroken periods of small-mind activity centered around completing tasks. A merciful awareness permeated our daily routine.

After twenty-some-odd years using the deep rock well, our water is still the best beverage we have to drink or offer our infrequent visitors. We bought large propane tanks and a gas refrigerator, stove, and freezer so that the house would be free of the hum and rattle of electric devices. We added a small gas heater as backup for our wood stoves and fireplace. We gathered piles of forest deadfall to dry and split. Various cut branches and split kindling lean against the adobe wall beside the oldest wood stove—our long winters warmed by the sun stacked beside the porch.

The well drilled, the septic tank dug and plumbed, we set up three solar arrays, no power or phone lines cutting through the forest. And after a few years we broke our resistance to being plugged into anything and bought a computer and a TV, which we connected to small satellite dishes. We were wide-screened hermits ready for the enveloping quiet.

Our mornings were full of grace. We usually woke early, our morning meditation begun when our eyes first opened by noting whether we awoke on the in-breath or out-breath so as to "awake when we awake," and slowly share whatever dreams we had on the previous night. A practice we continue to maintain.

It took awhile to become accustomed to the enveloping silence. To quiet the mind habitually crammed with expectation and habituation was yet another matter still. Our meditation practice gradually seeped into the chinks between restless thoughts.

The sound of wind and passing shadows of clouds, the coming and going of birds with the seasons became our backdrop, making a kind of visual music. There were no migrating visitors, no cars rushing by. The quiet was sinking in. This world fit just fine.

There is a boulder-strewn ridge that rises quickly from the forest just north of the house which serves as a pallet for innumerable contemplations. It changes from day to day. It has been over twenty-seven years, and we never weary of the great green kaleidoscope, the full green spectrum. The ponderosa tree tops are like shadow puppets dancing in the sunset halfway up the great red sandstone outcroppings.

On the gradual granite hillsides, there is white and rose quartz, and mica reflecting a thousand moons distributed along the path-side and across the flanks of the stream bank, settling into the unique, seemingly perfect patterns of nature in all its keen originality.

Settling into our forest home, we rarely went to town. A few people were confused, even insulted, by our lack of social interest. Indeed, over the years, only our children and some old friends, grandchildren, Ram Dass, and a few of our spiritual family have visited.

People occasionally asked how we could handle the silence, or each other, for 24/7. A friend from Boston asked, "How can you stand being out there in the middle of nowhere?" We laughed and answered, "Middle of nowhere? We aren't in the middle of nowhere; you are!"

For the first five years we had no phone in the house and instead, since we were still working with a few patients, asked if we might, once a week, use the phone in the general store seven miles away. After a few weeks, because of the delicate nature of some of the conversations with people in one sort of crisis or another, the very kind store owner said he would have a separate phone line installed in an unused four- by two-foot metal cabinet he would pull out of the back room so we could stick our heads in and talk in something that approached privacy. It was a sight for the locals to pass by our corner cabinet with our back ends hanging out, speaking in soft tones, even crying, with a parent who had just lost a child, or laughing with a friend whose child had just fed his new puppy the evening guest's éclair.

We feel blessed to have gotten the chance in this busy world to live, even a bit, like mountain hermits. Occasionally, Basho or Wang Wei drop by for a poem and a cup of fresh spearmint tea.

The Least Secret Teaching

For much of our life we have received remarkable teachings in how to be human beings from the animal spirits. It was their invitation that began our opening, and it remains that quality of wholeness experienced on this land that regulates the beat of our heart.

When I first heard someone say that in fifty years all the songbirds might be extinct, something trembled in the original song learned so long ago while sitting with a book in the backyard, listening. What would this world be like if there were no birds trilling truths from the ledge outside a frightened child's window, telling her that somehow everything is going to be okay, that we are each an integral part of something very big and indescribably beautiful?

What follows is nothing as exotic or romantic as the 125 species that migrated in and out of the wildlife sanctuary Stephen tended for The Nature Conservancy forty years ago, but the luminous essence remains nonetheless. Here are a few animal stories from our daily experience.

The Ladies

We built a chicken coop to house "the Ladies" in a comfortably warm space. Nests full of the communal clucking of brooding hens patrolled from the yard by the bright avian spark that is a Rhode Island Red rooster. Each morning we collected a few eggs in a wicker basket.

Among the colorful clutch of Polish Goldens, Araucanas (pastel eggs), Light Sussex, Marans, and Plymouth Rocks was one particularly large Rhode Island Red hen we called Big Red. Most chickens scatter when one walks through a group, but Big Red used to squat down and make herself a bit wider so that one would not pass her by without a pet on her soft clucking back.

Because of the deplorable conditions in egg factories, we adopted a few discarded White Leghorns, who had apparently stopped laying. Their beaks had been clipped short to allow severe overcrowding without causing injury to themselves or each other. Where their beak had been trimmed, it continued to grow into what resembled collagen lips. These were sad Leghorns with Betty Boop lips. After about a month of proper feed and nesting space, they began, quite happily, to lay again—golden eggs.

In the coop is the sound of heaven. Entering it we are surrounded, lifted into the pure cacophony, the soul music of the chickens' chorale. Then one morning, I entered the coop only to find a dozen chicks with their heads bitten off. Skunks!

Maintaining our responsibility to the skunks, in whose territory we had created a provocative chicken coop, rather than harming them, we began to yet further improve the fencing under which the skunks had apparently entered. Shoveling along the fence line most of the morning, we dug the fences deeper and buried a line of stones at its base to secure the area. Nothing short of a badger was going to dig its way into that enclosure!

But the next morning we found more headless chicks! We presumed the skunk had in some unlikely manner gone over rather than under the fence. We worked for most of the next day clumsily stretching sagging chicken wire across the top of the smaller pen. When our work was completed, we were sure those chicks remaining were at last safe. But next morning proved they were not.

We knew there were live traps large enough for a skunk, but there was a problem. While we could easily trap a skunk, it was the untrapping that could ruin your day! Stephen decided to sit out one night in the well-fenced chicken yard in hopes of uncovering their midnight access. He settled in beside the coop and, quieting his breath so as not to be discovered, sat quite still. He steadied his body in meditation and did not move in the least. This stillness was akin to a "vow sitting" done in the name of the hungry skunk of us all.

After perhaps an hour, Stephen arched his back to relieve pressure on his spine. Spreading wide his arms, he tilted his head back and looked up. The Southwestern sky was ablaze with a fiery Perseid meteor shower. A dozen streaks of light at a time stretched across the sky. Never had he seen such an extraordinary display. He was entranced by one streak of light after another, then five at a time, weaving an astral blanket across the sky.

Wanting to rest his arched neck, he looked back down. And there, not ten feet in front of him, was the skunk looking straight at him. It had slipped through what seemed far too slight an aperture between the corner post and the fence.

It was as beautiful as anything in creation. For a long moment, bathed together in a surreal star shower, they looked into each other's eyes. And beneath the star-loom sky they seemed simultaneously to bow and retreat.

Stephen returned with hammer and nails to secure the corner fencing.

The skunk went home and the sky kept on singing.

The Toads

Ten years ago, sitting under the starry river, we met a very large Colorado River toad. The female of the species is considerably larger, about four by seven inches and, not to be unkind, she probably weighed a substantial pound or two. Obviously, as the appellation goes, she was "one of God's creatures."

Visiting nightly, she was a creature unconstrained by boundaries and borderlines—once a tadpole, then an amphibian, a shape-shifting metamorphosis had happened in a wayside puddle attempting to outrun evaporation. She was now a land owner, a burrow usurper, night hunter along the Milky Way. And by day she was cold-blooded and followed the sun. But she couldn't outwit winter and we'd have to wait till spring to meet up with her again.

When she resurfaced, we built her a toad condo under an overhanging pinyon to honor the toad's predilection for shade. We overturned an old red clay flower pot with a broken rim and placed near her open door a shallow water-filled, hand-painted fish platter to act as her pool. It was a yellow-eyed, wide-mouthed, green-skinned Paradise.

Now talk about the difficulty in finding a mate! How was such an off-handed beauty going to find a lover hundreds of miles from the river of her namesake? But within four years she did. The racket that ensued from their lovemaking and later, from their teenage children getting in and out of the water to toughen their skin, emitting the Toady Tremolo that is described as a "low-pitched hoot" and a "croaka croak," became a constant reminder. But what were they reminding us of? Madame Toad, opening the Eye of Beauty, attempted to wake us to our Original Song. Her role in the food chain secure, bitter to the taste and touch, soft and vulnerable, she reminded us to tread gently, or as some tribal neighbors might say, "Walk in a sacred manner."

Now, every summer, the amphibious orchestra congregates like the Lenox School of Music at Tanglewood, rehearsing for a thirty-day performance before they hop up onto the warm stone path, mindful of the yellow eyes in the rock wall, under a recent moon.

Toward fall, playing a deadly game of "got ya," half a handful of toadlings loosely distribute around the garden on the ready to pursue bugs and grubs, crickets and mosquitoes, digging in the soft soil. In their individuation, they get a bit territorial. They sing a few songs for the well-being of us all, with hopes we can make it till spring.

Many did not make it, but those that survived were generations of focused and hardy, iridescent singers, caroling in a new season, the circle of life!

In an aging, empty, old pool we had built thirty years before to lure our grandchildren up onto the mountain, a small green-lively pond formed from the drought-precious remnants of rain water and snow melt has been dedicated to the support of the dwindling frog, toad, bat and, of course, bee population.

Toads sit like noted immortals at the edge of the water.
They just like a dip every once in a while
sing their heads off at night. What a holy racket!

In the peeling old pool a couple
of hundred gallons of lively swamp,
an oasis for the desaparacidos/the disappeared,
bees, bats, toads and frogs who think
they can catch liberation like a passing dragon fly.
A lone bat swooping over the inviting green ooze.

The Healing I Took Birth For

They sing the Mosquito Sutra these
Colorado River toads with big blue earrings.
Their hearts wide open.

Stories from Dr. Karlin

The planet consciousness in this once part of tribal lands is palpable. Living in our area, the native tribal peoples' intuitive interrelationship between animals and people has infiltrated the community consciousness.

"Do animals have Buddha nature?" Our veterinarian friend, Dr. Glenn Karlin, a clear-eyed Christian, told two stories. Though deeply imbued in his relationship to Christianity, he nonetheless told the story of "a raven come to take away the soul of a dying dog." He'd been called out of his clinic by a dog owner he had long known whose dog, a chow named Buster, he had often cared for. The dog lay dying in great pain from an automobile accident. "After leaning into the back of the SUV and talking to Buster for a while, about what a good dog he had been and how God loved him, I prepared a needle, and just as I was administering the final, fatal shot, a large raven, in a very unravenlike manner hovered over us, wings beating, just above the roof of the car. And when Buster breathed his last, the raven made a great animal sound and flew off with his soul."

Another time, Glenn said, he had treated a dog suffering from a long degenerative disease that eventually died. It was winter and the pet's dear friend said she wished to bury him on their land the following morning, so Dr. Karlin wrapped him with due honors and silent prayers to rest in peace for the night in the back of the SUV, until the morning burial. The woman told him that soon after parking the car behind the house she heard something of a ruckus and, peeking between the blinds, saw animals beginning to congregate around the back of the car. Coyotes, skunks, raccoons, and ravens. One might think that these carnivores were drawn to the smell of a dead animal, except that a raccoon or raven would never sit near a coyote or any of them near a skunk. They'd formed a semi-circle around the back of the car where the dog's body laid hidden from view, and they stayed there all night. At the first rays of sunrise, they all departed back into the forest.

White Clouds/ Blue Sky: Winter Hermitage

After the first snow, we go out searching for the music written in the crystal blanket.

Snow allows the invisible to be seen. What has unfolded under a moonless sky is exposed by dawn.

After the last storm, sitting on a high outcropping, we look down to see the winding, intersecting trails of mice hemming the fresh snow. A fugue. The long foot of a jack rabbit indifferently crisis-crossing the evidence of the hyperactive mouse's morning dash. A kettle drum punctuates the drifts. And near the bottom of the hill a bloodspot at the foot of the earthen dam and coyote tracks beside the opening of the rabbit's warren, Wagner in the wings.

In the afternoon, we see new tracks up on the mesa. The wild burro we heard last week has passed through once again. Following her unshod hoof prints, the wild runes of her midnight passing, disappearing on a sudden rock face where the snow has fallen away in the symbolic Pueblo Zia sun.

Finding near the top of the 700-foot incline, the continuation of the tracks of this burro lost from the herd, navigating by the stars. Down the ten-thousand-year-old deer trail, beneath the snow, are stone points and potsherds of pottery painted before the Conquistadors' deluge of European arrogance and brutal religion, after which they stopped painting their pots. These painted fragments mark the passing of whole continents of ourselves and all the tragedy it took to leave us so frightened and lost. Crossing the donkey's path, the broad spoor of a mountain lion follows its nose, as a solitary elk watches through a pagoda juniper.

Joining the procession, just behind the lion, following its tracks one-by-one through the snow, each species' track is deeper than the last, graphing evolution, and the food chain. The slow unfolding has an almost hypnotic effect. The pace slows, breath-after-breath, step-after-step, through the deep snow. The wind, a distant flute, raises a shimmering mist of snow; tablas on the inner ear.

Half blind, from looking so long into the glistening snow, the mind stops using words to think. And for a few moments, I can see, in images, how an animal thinks. Animals don't hear music, animals are music. When we observe them closely as Rodin reminded Rilke, it refines our seeing. He said, "Go to the zoo and learn how to see!" In the same way, the poem "The Panther and the Swan" was born. To see clearly is to open the eye of beauty, to hear with the inner ear, sitting quietly in the cave behind the ear's tympanum membrane, feeling, as much as hearing, the sounds unheard by most that fill the dark green paths of the animal world.

My breath becomes coordinated with each mouse and paw print. The breath is drawn in across the pure unruffled snow, and then drops exhaled, into the bottom of each perfect cougar print. The mind floats on the intersecting of the lion's breath and mine, as remnants of last night's dreams begin to surface.

One after another, submerged dreams arise then fade away melting at their edges like the prints followed into the sun. There is a song to be found in the hard breath of climbing, a rhythm in the blood that remembers. No one is born in a house. That comes later.

The puma has leapt up the rockslide to the top of the "cerro," and becomes the sky. Standing in the midst of the glistening snowfield, weeks of long-forgotten dreams come flooding through. Some have sprung from a vagrant thought or a milliwatt of fancy. Others had barely broken the surface and sunk back down waiting to get born, even those that were born against their will. Lovely dreams stack like prayer cloths waiting to comfort devotees ascending and descending from the storehouse of dreams, revealing the astounding contents of the heart.

Dissolving out of our tracks too left in the snow, smiling at nature's absurd perfection standing in the midst of a snow field, I shake my head at "human kind and unkind." Present to the terrible/wonderful unfolding of creation and destruction, in the push and pull of gravity, in the brilliant turmoil of the stars.

The lion's steamy breath and the thin whistle of the frigid mouse are brought home to be entrusted to a poem, that place which is the altar of the heart, where precious memories reside in honor and gratitude. And when the heart and mind are in harmony, the flowers of humility can be offered on the breathing alter.

Blue sky/white snow.

The Mad Raven Teachings

What do you do with the resident raven's fledgling, now full grown with some sort of brain anomaly that causes it to caw loudly every few seconds, twenty times a minute, for weeks, sometimes quite near the house for hours, often outside your bedroom window as early as 5:30 a.m.?

One can feel the gut tighten with resistance to the long repetition beginning once again. Then mindfulness softens from caw to caw.

In the course of reflecting on possible solutions, we recalled an experiment many years ago in Japan, when with the most sophisticated electroencephalograms, they measured brain reactions to long-repeated stimuli. The recurring ringing of a bell was noticed in the ordinary mind to slowly diminish in reaction, as habituation to the stimuli occurred within a very few minutes. After a while they hardly noticed it. But when advanced students of Zen, and even more so Zen masters, were thus measured, it was noticed that each time the bell was rung, no matter how many times, the same spiking of a mindful response could be detected. Zen students and masters did not habituate, did not take bells (or life) for granted, but were completely present for each succeeding moment.

Could we use raven-caw to bring us closer to the moment instead of following the ordinary aversion to uncontrollable, even unpleasant repetition?

At times, when quiet and present, we could receive the sound with no resistance and even a considerable concern for the bird's well-being. But when we were focused elsewhere, it became an unwelcome intrusion. What at first was resisted by fear and aversion was gradually surrendered to with mercy and awareness. Like any healing, when what turned to suffering is revealed and entered, the long abandoned is called home. Even now I hear our poor brain-damaged ward heading this way down the valley.

Months ago, when we first heard the calling, we thought the bird would probably die soon from whatever birth defect caused its unusual behavior. Yet here it comes now, calling out in its own way, "Karuna, Karuna" (compassion compassion) as did Huxley's birds on his ideal island. And settling on a nearby branch it echoes those long-lost birds, "Here and Now, Boys! Here and Now!"

It reminds us to soften, and that some questions, particularly those that deal directly with life, have no answer. That sometimes even love can't readily find a way.

Never was the need for surrender clearer or the fact that to honor the Buddha is to wash the feet of all sentient beings.

When the Owl Calls Your Name, It's Your Turn in the Dentist's Chair

Coming into town, the animal spirit teachings continue to apply. Waiting to have two extractions in the dentist's office, I remembered kneeling by the side of the road years before, unsuccessfully attempting to loosen the wing feathers of a dead great horned owl, for an artful shamanic project. Pulling as hard as I could without crushing the feathers, they wouldn't budge. Then I was reminded of the Native American Way, the Original Way of respect and interconnectedness with creation. I stopped exerting such force on the long flightless wing and instead respectfully asked its permission to remove the feathers. I bowed to it. When I tried again to extract the powerful feathers, they slipped effortlessly into my palm. So, sitting in the dentist's office, I gave permission to those two old teeth to go on their destined way, to let go. And so they did. I wonder if the Tooth Fairy knows what a dead owl has to teach us.

On this beautiful morning, there was a mountain lion on the hillside behind the house, and a lion in the heart, behind the body.

SIXTEEN

Gratitude Grows in the
Ripening Heart

TODAY IS A DAY of a week of a month of a year of a lifetime of thankfulness for what has been and what will be. Gratitude for the love I have experienced as importantly as the loving kindness I may have given. I am grateful for this life in which we continue to feel our way toward the truth. Grateful that gratitude has found us where we live.

Grateful for this very instant, this moment of awareness to which my heart is drawn—grateful for time and timelessness, for the Presence in presence. Grateful for friends who remind me of love, and for those who do not, who remind me of how unloving I can be.

Remembering throughout the day, how wishful thinking eludes this precious moment and excludes a world of possibilities, returning to gratitude for all I have learned and how precious the opening has become. Grateful for what the past has taught me and my ability to not stop there. Grateful to go beyond what I know into the future unknown where all growth occurs; grateful for being a bit more alive each day.

Just a Little Bit Older and More Graceful on the Path[1]
When we settled into this land, the little ponderosa behind the rear porch was two-and-a-half feet tall, now it is over twenty feet. When

---

1 Parts drawn from *Turning Toward the Mystery*

we moved here, Stephen was 5' 9"; now he's 5' 8". I was a bit further away from the land; now I'm a bit closer. Gravity's slide rule brings us all to ground.

On most days our gratitude to life, to love, to spiritual practice, grows. And the birds whose names, age insists, I have to relearn each spring come to teach us devotion and humility, surrender, and impermanence.

Aging can be "one insult after another" for those looking for a loophole in the Law of Impermanence, an insult to those who long to maintain a self-image which so often caused them discomfort. Unfinished business raises our blood pressure and lowers our self-esteem. Those who felt life was an endless series of rehearsals and job interviews often feel like an unwelcome guest at their own table.

Or aging can be the chance of a lifetime. Less entangled in fear and loathing, in sickness, old age, and death because, in the process of aging, the life-force gradually withdraws from our peripheries and becomes focused in the heart. For this reason, spiritual work, in the later years, can often be the most fruitful and satisfying of one's life. The spirit is more accessible in this great indwelling than perhaps at any other time. Liberation is never so available. We reread the books and seek the influences that propelled our evolution. We explore the art of aging, or we suffer an even greater fear of death.

Aging is a process of gestation, a spiritual option. It is not a slow death, but a crucial part of our unending birth. Though the body may be getting a bit loose on the bones, the heart can be like a mountain growing less distant each day.

In the process of aging, the energy of the body (chi, shakti) gradually withdraws into the heart. That's why I feel spiritual work, in the later years, can often be the most productive of one's life. The spirit is more accessible in this great indwelling than perhaps at any other time. Lightenment, perhaps possibly enlightenment, has never been so available.

When the body can no longer support it, there is a gathering of the life energy in the heart which, it is said, rises as death approaches like a fountain from the crown of the skull.

In aging, a gradual, rather than rapid, accumulation of the light in the birth chamber of the heart gives rise to a sense of even greater aliveness.

Most of our friends have gone on ahead. We read them the sutras and the Bhagavad Gita. We practice dying. Our prayers are the simplest and the truest. Death is not an enemy.

Father Bede Griffiths, a spiritual seeker throughout his remarkable life, said he learned more in the last two years of his life than he did in the first eight-four.

Though I know that death is not so different than life, just a change in lifestyle perhaps, it is still different enough to take me away from my loved ones, and I grieve the very thought of it.

Passing through an old New England graveyard, we saw a weathered stone that said:

Remember friends as you pass by as you are now so once was I
as I am now so you must be prepare yourself to follow me.

It is said that to be fully alive we need to stop postponing death. That works well on the meditation pillow, but in the hospital or the doctor's office, it is quite another matter. Even for those who have fortunately, usually through hard work, experienced what is referred to as "deathlessness," there are still remnants of our deeply conditioned fear of death, and the concept of Judgment Day, not to mention the apparently inborn fear of "not being," which no belief in an afterlife can prepare one for.

And, of course, much of our fear of death may well contain a substantial fear of dying, of the pain and dismay that might accompany the process of the body falling away. This naturally preceding whatever comes next, be it call waiting or a dial tone, the arms of a loved one, or, dying on a lucky day, the luminous peace of "the Deathless."

As the Song Echoes in the Dome
of the Skull It Sets the Fontanel Ablaze

Lighter than the thoughts on whose surface the world is mirrored like a dream,
consciousness continues into uncharted territory, expanding outward into evolution.

Rising from the top of the head, an ecstatic devotion sweeps through the universe that
blesses even invisible realms.

And at the center of the song a silence so deep
that form cannot manifest...

It is the silence which precedes God and the Word.
Time and silence going beyond, going altogether beyond.

Nothing we have learned is of any use because there is nothing to control. Wild wisdom converges from the ten directions. Unencumbered by reason, it discloses how even suffering fits perfectly into the scheme of things. Beyond pleasure and pain we see how our attachment to each other attracts incarnations from across time. Leaving all else behind, rapture follows the light.

There is nowhere else to go, nothing else to do or be. No truth greater than "the open secret," waiting to be known, resting in the Clear Light that greets the dying and the fully born, that only love survives. In timelessness, beyond ourselves, we remember time and the focal point through which we passed on our way home and around.

Several decades after he left his old cabin in the redwoods, Stephen, as an experiment in conscious aging, returned to "my mountain." Climbing the old mountain he knew so well, he said the trail seemed longer without Noah's small hand in his, without Tara picking flowers as they gradually climbed.

But the vague evening deer and the shimmering morning lupine had not forgotten and greeted him with wonder. His feet washed, blessed by the river he crossed through. The forest returned his prayers for their well-being, reminding him of the wild flowers that used to grow from a discarded sandal and the bobcats that nestled in the milk case by the old sequoia.

He found his way up to where his shadow waited patiently for his return. Angels and ghosts had set a friendly table. There was nourishment for his journey already waiting by the door for him to get going further up the mountain, past the tree line, up where there are a few poems Basho did not write that he left for us. . . .

Momentary Diamond

I am just an innocent bystander attending the passing show with an increasing capacity for mercy and loving kindness. Not judging or embarrassed by the pain we are in but softening to allow some etheric element to surface long enough to recognize our true way home.

This softening opens the body-mind. Holding nothing back from our uninjured grace, our natural loves and inclinations, our connection with sentience in whatever form, we stop becoming and settle into being. We are not other than That.

From this perspective no inner or outer, no endings or beginnings, momentary diamond. When the heart comes to the surface even goals can become obstacles. When anything other than love, or at least an active presence, is our pole star we may continually feel lost. This perspective of the uninjured and uninjurable qualities of Being is capable of revealing the watcher and the watched as simple eternities.

In a quiet out breath the uninjurable background comes forward and the mind succumbs to a peace that wants nothing more than mercy and loving kindness for all sentient beings and most notably, surprisingly, our slow moving selves.

When we steady ourselves on the tight rope, coming into balance, afflictive emotions quieting, mind settling down; like the stone rolled from the mouth of the cave the opening heart taking the wheel we become, as one person put it, "the dance partner for angels," our song heard between the waves. Even in the face of a hurricane, the loss of a loved one, illness, the disappearance of faith, there is something present that supports the "still small voice within," the slight, but gradually increasing hum of the uninjured, the inborn cipher for what some call "the voice of God" and others refer to as "the enormity or the vastness of Being."

When I watch the mind manifest, as thoughts, feelings, sensations come and go and I allow the passing show to just move across the mind screen like waves across the ocean of consciousness and letting go, indeed letting it all "come and go," I encourage the vastness of awareness by which I see to predominate. As what can be said to be distractions by some is recognized by what in Zen can be referred to as "mind only." Just the passing show we mistake for ourselves but is actually the mechanical unfolding of the normal unkempt mind.

When somewhat out of balance nearly anything can knock us over, the frown of a stranger, the wrong flavor, a stubbed toe. Pain becomes suffering due to resistance. Resistance is the unwillingness to be present, a trembling in the desire not to be, a dark wave across the Reservoir of Grief.

To cultivate consciousness of the uninjured is to find our true and original nature, our natural way through. When the world, or even the body, is at war, but the heart's practice is gradually approaching peace on the daily path of mindfulness, the labyrinth of life and particularly mind-body difficulties become workable.

Born into this body, to discover what limits our joy (imagining ourselves something smaller) and certainly our happiness (lost in the furls of desire), we miss the boundless clarity of our underlying nature.

Epilogue

"WHO AM I TO be writing a book about devotion and mindfulness when any number of my spiritual comrades might well do a better job?" To speak with true confidence about Who and What, about When and Where, is beyond me. But I can meditate and sing, contemplate and chant, and I feel the *dharma* in my bones. It is only from here, incomplete as it may be, that I can begin to undertake such a book as this which attempts to show how mindfulness practice and devotional yogas complement and strengthen each other.

Each practice, whether seeking our original song or essential mind, follows the inner travelogues of our pilgrimage, between a near comatose forgetfulness and the ever-widening entrance to the enormity of Being.

It feels as though anything of value that I might write must have been said before. Clarity, though sometimes breath-taking, is also immediately obvious and available throughout time from the timeless.

Sometimes it seems as though I am at the end of a long line of thought repeated across time until it appeared again in some crevice of my wandering mind. And how many indeed have said exactly this!

I look at the page like a weaver contemplates a freshly strung loom, while restless in the drawer, an anxious shuttle conjures images and observations by the basket-full. Though we don't quite know who we are, when we know the direction we are traveling, we trust we will find out. There is no use asking directions, when genuine truth is to be found, as Kabir says, "in the breath inside the breath." With a single natural breath, horizonless, we share a sacred suchness. But to speak knowingly, whether as object or subject, whether in the first person or about original personage, is quite another matter.

Freed, this joy is present in many who have surrendered, with no force or reinforcement of unhappiness, their unhappiness. Recognizing that happiness is a myth, but joy is our birthright, there is a sense of fulfillment. Liberation. What I pay homage to is not old gods or revered gurus, but our essential nature, the Being in being, the heart of the matter.

When I began my life review due to the insistence by a leading physician that I probably had only a few months or a year at most to live, I thought it was time to implement a reappraisal of all that had gone before. A finishing of unfinished business. A tying up of loose ends. A more thorough engagement of forgiveness and gratitude.

And a remarkable melding of my beloved and me entering each other's experience to speak wholeheartedly of our own.

When told I was about to lose all I loved, naturally, I was depressed. Stuck in the quicksand of helplessness and self-pity, I needed a skillful means of pulling myself free. A way of re-engaging my illness with my years of spiritual practice to help myself get loose of my holding, soften my belly, and open my heart to the cancer. Even forgive the body for being in so much discomfort and accept the various aspects of fear that compete for my attention. But entering directly the sensations/symptoms, I gradually began to move through the painful stage of fear and resistance that often precedes the open vistas of acceptance.

In the taking of notes about the unfolding of my process, I undertook an exploration of the debris and the incompleteness of the trail I left behind me. I appraised what limited access to the heart of the matter and how one might open that heart in hell, by increasing the introduction of kindness instead of judgment into the merciful passage of our long-feared, mythical Judgment Day. Balancing the loving kindness that steadies the mind and eases the body. Exploring the adverse reaction to illness as well as clarity's ability to break such addiction by uprooting the long-conditioned impulse to escape rather than respond to distress. Employing the power to soften to physical and mental discomfort instead of hardening in reaction to our fear and loathing. Even remembering the mercy we took birth for and the kindness even to ourselves that awaits in our next mindful breath.

A life review can be strong medicine to revive the body and awaken the mind to the preciousness of the moment that then draws our attention into the area most calling for healing.

✳

Attention heals

Looking into, exploring, even investigating moment-to-moment discomfort with a merciful awareness softens the tension that exacerbates pain and turns it to suffering.

I think this writing is a healing tool that was long called for by my resistance to my present condition. It beseeched me to look it in the eyes and respect it for what it was, entering it with mindfulness and loving kindness.

My clear intentions were to do my illness no harm (not heating it up with a homicidal revenge and reactive resistance, but only cooling it down with a merciful acceptance and kind-heartedness) only to send it on a long-overdue pilgrimage of forgiveness and kind self-awareness that perhaps might offer respite from the hard times of late. To approach with mercy that which we have mercilessly attempted to escape from our whole lives.

Illness, even a recent wound, can remind us of the same old pain that is the legacy of our age-old forgetfulness of the uninjured and uninjurable truth within us that wants us only to be whole. Much of our pain is homesickness.

One of the lessons from this process had to do with the mystery of why we are here in the first place: to take ourselves into our own hearts as if we were our only child, to find a deeper level of joy and watch change with a soft belly. And love for no reason in particular.

Mother-of-us-all prays to free us
from our image of perfection
to which so much suffering clings.

When in the shadowy mind
we imagine ourselves imperfectly,
praying to be freed by enlightenment,
she refines our prayers.

Putting her arms around us
she bids us rest our head on her shoulder
whispering, don't you know
with all your fear and anger
all you are fit for is love.

Epilogue into the Present

Tara: Memories of Momma Dre (really *Mom* to me) go back almost as far as I can remember. The first time we met, it was in a small rented home my Dad had in Santa Cruz, and he came back excited from a retreat telling my younger brother, Noah, and I that he had met his true love and soul mate, Ondrea. She lived in an adobe in Taos, New Mexico ("what is that?? And WHERE is that?!" I thought). The fear that overcame me doesn't resonate today, but I knew at eleven years old that things were going to change—and quickly. She came to visit in Santa Cruz and was very kind—I have an initial memory of thinking, "Wow—she has really nice hair." She was loving and compassionate towards me and things moved quickly with Dad and "O" establishing their lives together; Dad was moving to New Mexico to be with her and her son James, who would become my new older brother. Was she the enemy or my most amazing Angel sent to protect and guide me? At that time I didn't know how to feel— I was scared and angry. My Dad was leaving (the most stable influence in the time of uncertainty and insanity in my young life), and although he wanted me to go with him, I felt I had to stay back in Santa Cruz and care for my younger brother and sister (twins), and try to hold things together with the chaos of growing up with my bio Mom—and all that came with it. Growing up far too fast for my age and encountering situations that would most definitely shape choices and decisions I made as I became an "adult," which in my recollection began at age eight when the twins were born and I took over many responsibilities. I know Dad and Momma Dre wanted to protect me, but I had protecting to do of my own and I wasn't ready to leave Santa Cruz and the twins yet.

I remember the drive from Santa Cruz to Santa Fe, where they settled, in the big blue '70s van with Dad and Noah and calling Momma Dre to tell her we were running a day or so late—a "trick" to surprise her and just show up (yes—I did the dirty work). And then there we were, and the love between them as these families, parents, children, siblings, pasts, and the present began to meld together to create a family.

Various visits throughout the years to see Dad and fam created more and more open communication and trust with Momma Dre, laughter and silliness and understanding of what LOVE could and SHOULD be between adults. It wasn't always easy, but I never considered her a "stepmother"—she was always a friend, confidant, and supporter—even when I didn't know how extremely valuable that would be as my life journey took me through some very dark, danger-ous, and unstable paths. She was and has always been there for me without judgment and with unending support and understanding. What an amazing gift to be bestowed by one life to another human being—I most definitely would not be the woman, mother, friend, business owner, and have the understanding of unconditional love if it wasn't for Momma Dre. There is no doubt in my mind, heart, and soul that without her influence I would be less of a person.

I moved to Taos in 1984 when the toll of growing up in Santa Cruz and the chaos of my "childhood" had finally taken its toll on my tender, yet hardened heart at fifteen years old, and I took the plunge to move to Taos, New Mexico. What a complete culture shock from being on the beach; the oldest; not many boundaries and me assuming the role of parent for the twins and my mother! It was quite a change, to say the least. There are teenage ups and downs and I was now in a family situation that required boundaries and rules—whaaaaat??? It was all done with love and clarity, but a major transition nonetheless. Our bond strengthened over the years and Momma Dre was happy to have a girl around to have time with after being surrounded by all the boys for many years, and I finally had a mother figure that acted with protection, direction, and understanding. It was a lovely match between us and many times of laughter and love that will always remain a private bond between mother and daughter.

When I think of Mom, she is to me a constant companion, con-fidant, never-ending cheerleader, boastful mother, best friend, giggly teenager when we act like we are in high school (which is quite fun), wise teacher, protector, and most blessed Goddess that was brought into my life by a relationship—falling in love with Dad, and he with her—a true and enduring love I can only hope to emulate someday.

And from Noah: I love you, Momma Ondrea. You gave me the greatest gift possible: life, love, and the Dharma. You saved my life.

About Ondrea Levine

Ondrea Levine has over the past forty-five years been skillfully working with the dying and grieving, the last thirty-seven years together with her beloved Stephen. They have worked together on numerous books and with many hundreds of people in the process of letting go of their life, acting as a guide through their process, sitting bedside encouraging their life review (as she has here shared hers), sharing the process of shedding the traumas of a lifetime on the way to shedding their body; while also working with coma patients, teaching meditation, and a natural taking of the world into her heart in effortless contemplations.

Ondrea brings back the perennial teachings of wisdom, mercy, and service as a means to seeing clearly and being present to the world within, and about, us. Liberating in oneself insight into a world crying for our clarity and healing.

Emerging from the depths of a hard-fought half-life, breaching the surface to offer that which had ground her smooth, offering teachings in insight practice, the purifying cultivation of forgiveness and the finishing of business. Working on the Apology Page from the *www.LevineTalks.com* site, she offers the possibility of shedding some of the detritus accumulated in our forgetfulness.

The teachings found in her book *The Healing I Took Birth For* have offered many "a way through." A rough map to the healing that is deeper than cure. And perhaps the rebirthing we took birth for.

Stephen Levine is Ondrea's husband and spiritual partner. Half of the shared heart each equally makes reference to. He is the author of several books.

To Our Readers

Weiser Books, an imprint of Red Wheel/Weiser, publishes books across the entire spectrum of occult, esoteric, speculative, and New Age subjects. Our mission is to publish quality books that will make a difference in people's lives without advocating any one particular path or field of study. We value the integrity, originality, and depth of knowledge of our authors.

Our readers are our most important resource, and we appreciate your input, suggestions, and ideas about what you would like to see published.

Visit our website at *www.redwheelweiser.com* to learn about our upcoming books and free downloads, and be sure to go to *www.redwheelweiser.com/newsletter* to sign up for newsletters and exclusive offers.

You can also contact us at *info@rwwbooks.com* or at
Red Wheel/Weiser, LLC
665 Third Street, Suite 400
San Francisco, CA 94107